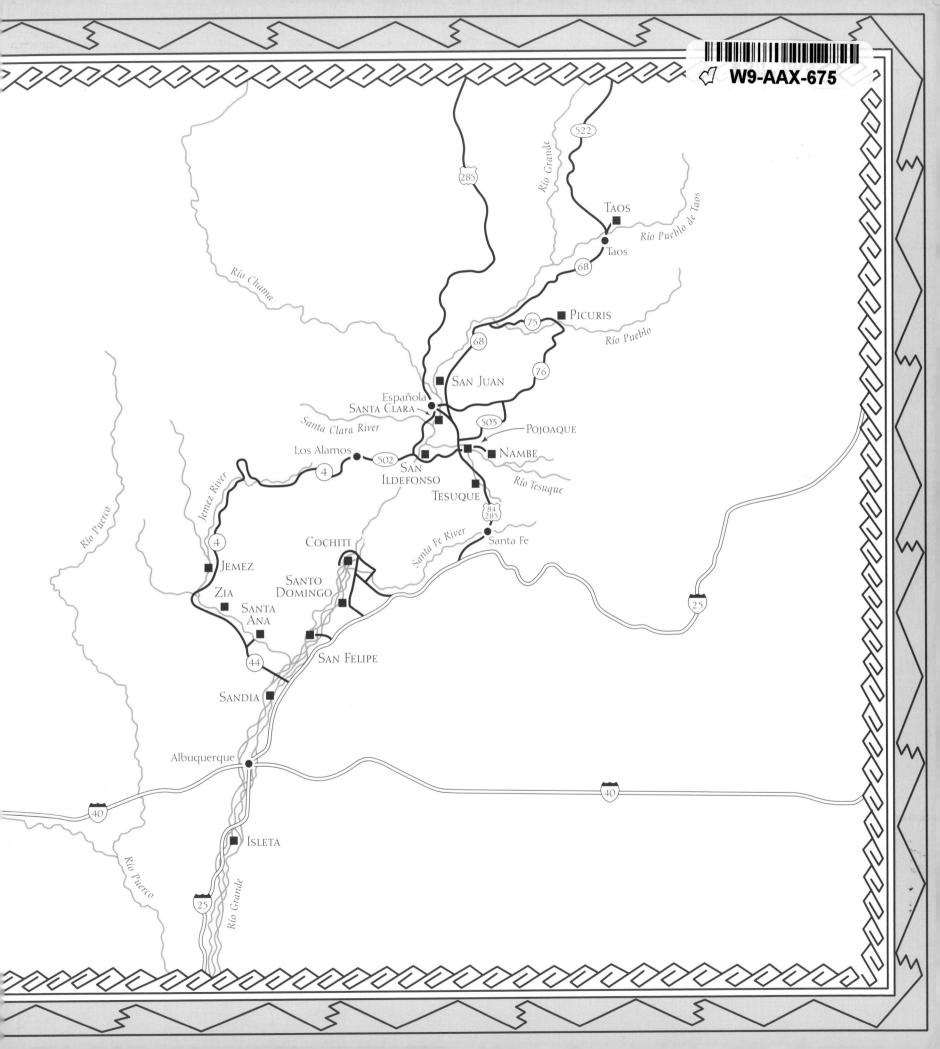

W9-AAX-675

PUEBLO PEOPLE

PUEBLO PEOPLE

Ancient Traditions Modern Lives

MARCIA KEEGAN

Foreword by Regis Pecos
Preface by Joe S. Sando

Clear Light Publishers

Santa Fe

Dedicated to my Pueblo Indian friends with love

Acknowledgments

This book would not have been possible without help from many people. I want to thank, first, all those friends who allowed me to photograph them over the years, as well as those who supported me in preparing this book. Chief among these latter are my husband, Harmon Houghton, and Carole and Jerry Shaff. I am grateful to my editor and long-time friend, Valerie Shepherd; to Carol O'Shea for her typography and production; and to Benjamin Koo for his taking extra care to ensure quality printing. I thank Regis Pecos for his Foreword, which touched me deeply, and Joe S. Sando for his insightful Preface. In addition, Joe S. Sando, Howard Bryan, and Leon Roybal provided editorial assistance for which I am deeply grateful.

Clear Light Publishers, 823 Don Diego, Santa Fe, New Mexico 87501
WEB: www.clearlightbooks.com

Royalties in part will benefit the Santa Fe Indian School, owned by the All Pueblo Indian Council.

First Edition
10 9 8 7 6 5 4 3 2 1

Library of Congress Cataloging-in-Publication Data

Keegan, Marcia.
        Pueblo people : ancient traditions modern lives / by Marcia Keegan
            p.   cm.
        ISBN 1-57416-000-1
        1. Pueblo Indians.   2. Pueblo Indians—Pictorial works.
    I. Title.
    E99.P9K435   1998
    978.9004'974—dc21   98-30832
                                                             CIP

Front & Back Cover: Bernice Roybal Martinez with her grandfather, Juan Cruz Roybal,
    San Ildefonso Pueblo
Frontispiece: Comanche dancers returning to the kiva, San Ildefonso Pueblo
Design: Marcia Keegan
Production & Typography: Carol O'Shea
Map: Deborah Reade
Color Separations by Rainbow Digicolor Inc., Toronto
Printed and Bound in Hong Kong by Book Art Inc., Toronto.

Contents

Foreword *by Regis Pecos*

Executive Director of the State of New Mexico Office of Indian Affairs

The songs, the dances as taught by the Ancient Ones continue...

This book is a profoundly beautiful piece of art and a gift as timeless as the Pueblo People. Marcia Keegan's life work reveals what few, if any, photographers have ever captured: the reflection in the eyes of the Pueblo people of a sacred trust of friendship that is equal to the spectacular beauty of the special and beloved places they have shared with her. The book is a story in photographs of a journey that few non-Pueblo people have been allowed to travel. It is a journal of friends who share with Marcia insight into their lives, their homes, their communities, and their homelands. Through these faces and places, the story is told that the spirit of the Ancient Ones lives on in the lives of the Pueblo people today, and that the journey of the people continues.

As we observe the Quatrocentenario—the 400th anniversary of the coming of Europeans to our land, an event that would forever change our world—this book is a timely reminder of our endurance, our perseverance, our struggle for survival. It reminds us all that we are truly blessed to still have what defines us as Pueblo people: our songs, our dances, our religion, our language, our families, our homelands. We have these only because those who went before us resisted compromising their way of life so that we could inherit all that defines who we are as a people. Marcia, as no one else before her, captures in her photos the love, respect, and compassion that are the foundation of Pueblo values.

For us as Pueblo people, this wonderfully beautiful book should remind us of the awesome responsibility we have to do as our forefathers have done. We must preserve this way of life so that our children's children and their children and all those who follow will be born into a world that gives them value and meaning in their lives. Only in this way can they share the universal principles of love, respect, and compassion with all those who cross their paths in this journey of life. In this way, when we adhere to the tenets of Pueblo philosophy and the Pueblo way of life, the Ancient Ones will be proud that the spirit and endurance of our people live in the hearts and minds of the young. Then the rest of the world may take these seeds of love, respect, and compassion and plant and nurture them to nourish their spirit.

During our long deliberations to determine what we must do to commemorate the 400th anniversary, we were reminded by one of the elders of the Tribal Council of Santo Domingo that no matter what history reflects, we cannot afford to teach our children to hate.

Through her love, respect, and compassion, Marcia Keegan exemplifies in this book the ultimate beauty in life and the gift of friendship.

Preface *by Joe S. Sando*

Director of Pueblo Indian Research and Study Center
Indian Pueblo Cultural Center

During my researching days I went to the Smithsonian Institution in Washington, D.C., to look for photographs of Pueblo Indian people. I was shown a drawer labeled "Southwest." My task was made easier by the fact that it turned out to be only New Mexico Indians. The photographs were of Apache, Navajo, and Pueblo Indians.

I quickly separated the Apache and Navajo pictures from the Pueblo photographs. These were mainly of Santa Clara and Zuni people taken in the 1880s and later. Most gave no name or other identification of the subjects and often the photographers were unknown. We later learned that some of these early photographers were A. C. Vroman, Edward Curtis, Charles Lummis, and Simeon Schwemberger. Laura Gilpin arrived on the scene a little later. These were the friendlier photographers; others were rude and demanding, so much so that the Pueblo people turned against allowing further photography.

It is against this background that Marcia Keegan arrived on the pueblo scene. She began taking photographs in the pueblos thirty years ago and has gained the friendship of the Pueblo people of New Mexico. Her photography books, including Enduring Culture and Mother Earth, Father Sky, may have introduced her to many Indian people as a friendly person. Her calendars with photographs of New Mexico Indian people and scenes have become a favorite of Pueblo children in their classrooms.

For many years the interest in Indians of the East and Midwest led to the neglect of the Pueblo people. Keegan's books give close-up views of our people and culture, and help outsiders understand the Pueblo way of life. This book should gain appreciative readers now and in the years ahead.

Introduction

I've been photographing my friends, the Pueblo people, for over thirty years. The opportunity to do this evolved rather naturally out of sharing the events of our daily lives. People I've had the good fortune to know invited me to their homes where I ate chile stew and bread pudding, or they visited my home to dine on barbecue. We've exchanged news and recipes, political opinions, and complaints about the weather; we've been together at weddings, birthdays, funerals, and graduations. Elders have offered their wise advice and told me stories of the past, and the children have allowed me to share their play. Over the years I've watched these children grow up, encounter the world, and have children of their own. This book is a record of these friendships and is, in essence, like a family album.

As I sorted through my photographs to compose this book, I found that in some cases I selected several pictures of a single person and four generations of a single family at various ages. There are a number of pictures of celebrations, as these have been high points in our lives. These occasions include traditional feast days and community events such as the original and anniversary celebrations of the return of Taos Pueblo's sacred Blue Lake.

Just as in many family albums, the pictures in this book show people readily consenting to their portrait. They acknowledge the camera, just as most relatives and friends do when we take the photographs that document the passage of our lives together. The portraits are a joint undertaking of the person photographed and the photographer, with full acknowledgment of the contribution of each of us to the process.

After many years of being often-unwilling subjects of hordes of photographers, most Pueblo people have restricted or carefully defined non-Indians' use of cameras and sketching on the pueblos. If there is power in images (and the

Pueblo people and I share the belief that there is), the Pueblos "took back the power" of their own images by making such restrictions. I have always honored these restrictions when and where they were imposed; to not do so would violate our friendship, just as ignoring a friend's heartfelt request would damage the mutual trust on which the friendship is founded.

I strongly urge visitors to pueblos today to honor any restrictions on photography or sketching. It is part of the covenant that we as guests of the Pueblos should honor to show our respect for their traditions and their desire for privacy.

Many of the pueblos that do not permit photography do allow photographs to be made of people in their homes—with their consent, of course. For this reason, many of the photographs from the stricter pueblos, such as Santo Domingo, were taken indoors. Also in this book are photographs of dances that may no longer be photographed; these pictures were made before the restrictions were imposed. Also, there are photographs in the book depicting several pueblos now closed to photography; again, the pictures were taken before the bans were enacted.

I am grateful to have had the opportunity to make records of these places, people, and events over the years, especially of those that may no longer be documented. I was fortunate to have been able to photograph people such as the now-widely known potter Maria Martinez of San Ildefonso, and to photograph Governor Robert Lewis of Zuni both as a young man and shortly before his death. I feel blessed to share these images of my many friends with a world that hopes to better understand these unique and wonderful people. This book is both my life's work and a celebration, with love and caring, of my friends' lives. This is their book.

Marcia Keegan

The Pueblo people of New Mexico live today in nineteen autonomous villages scattered over the northern half of the state. "Pueblo" is the Spanish word for village or town, and sixteenth century Spanish explorers first referred to these community dwellers as Pueblo Indians. At that time there may have been as many as eighty such villages throughout the region. Pueblo Indians of today, as well as the village-dwelling Hopi Indians of northern Arizona, are sovereign nations that trace their ancestries through various groups of early cultures that inhabited the American Southwest long before the nomadic Navajo or Apache Indians migrated into the region. Pueblo Indians do not have a common language, but are divided into five linguistic groups. Most, however, are bilingual, speaking English as well as their native tongues.

Early efforts to stamp out their religions were resisted by the Pueblo people, and the Pueblos today practice a unique blend of Christian and Native religions. A central feature of each pueblo is a mission church; some of the churches date back to the seventeenth century, when they were constructed under the supervision of Franciscan friars. Native religion and culture find expression today in the traditional ceremonial dances performed on the spacious open plaza in the center of each pueblo. Many of the annual feast day ceremonial dances are open to the public. Rituals of the traditional Pueblo religion are private and take place in enclosed chambers called kivas.

Traditional Pueblo government, which has existed for many centuries, is the most enduring form of local government in America. Each pueblo has its own self-governing body and officials, and is represented in the All Indian Pueblo Council.

Ancestral Homes

Canyon de Chelly petroglyph

Three Rivers petroglyph

Kuaua pictograph

Chaco Canyon

Bandelier

Mesa Verde

Aztec

Canyon de Chelly

Kuaua

Puye

Pecos

Gila

Three Rivers

Three Rivers petroglyphs

Chaco Canyon

The Pueblo Indian people of the southwestern United States are as indigenous as Americans can be, having lived among the rugged mountains, dry mesas, and cottonwood-lined rivers for thousands of years. The culture they maintain today, with its earthen houses, strong family and community ties, and rituals evoking the mystical connection between all things, is one that evolved naturally and gradually as a response to life in the landscape.

Some 2,000 years ago, a group known as the Hohokam (O'Odham) settled the area of what is now southern Arizona, where they practiced advanced irrigation techniques. Others whom anthropologists call the Mogollon settled in the mountains in southern New Mexico as early as 300 B.C. The Mimbres branch of these people produced beautiful pottery with animal and anthropomorphic designs. Eventually settlements spread throughout the Southwest, including its northern regions and parts of Utah, Arizona, Colorado, and New Mexico. As time went on the populations of these groups swelled until thousands of villages dotted the land and tens of thousands of people farmed the red earth, and hunted, fished, traded, and shared their innovations under the blue desert sky.

The Pueblo people are conscious of the long ties of time that link them to the ancestors they call the Ancient Ones. (Pueblo people prefer not to use the term Anasazi, which is a Navajo word meaning "enemies of our ancestors" and is therefore pejorative.) The sedentary cultures of the Ancient Ones developed in the Southwest from the Desert Archaic Culture group, which practiced hunting and gathering. The new cultures at first lived in pithouses dug into the ground, with above-ground walls made of poles and brush plastered with mud. They had no pottery, but their weaving arts, especially basketmaking, were highly developed, and for this reason these early groups of Native Americans are referred to as Basketmakers.

By A.D. 700 their houses evolved into completely above-ground dwellings made of slumped adobe or of mud-covered stone, entered through the roofs via ladders. These gradually became more elaborate, until the people began to make the rooms contiguous and build room atop room, leaving terraces that they used as workspaces and using some interior rooms for storage and others as living spaces. These multistoried dwellings were America's first apartment houses. Later they

Left: Kiva at Pecos Ruins
Below: Zuni pictographs
Right: Gila Cliff Dwellings

were built around a central plaza. Kivas, subterranean or semisubterranean structures used for communal ceremonial purposes, began to appear between A.D. 900 and 1100.

The people developed pottery, and they intensified their agricultural practices, still living on some wild foods, but also cultivating corn, beans, and squash. The style of pottery and the new building style are the indicators used by archaeologists to define these people as Pueblo, the Spanish word for these apartment-house villages.

A good example of the Ancient Ones' building is preserved at the Gila Cliff Dwellings National Monument in southwestern New Mexico, built approximately A.D. 1270 and abandoned in the early 1300s.

The most spectacular and best-preserved dwellings are their ruins at Chaco Canyon, New Mexico, and Mesa Verde, Colorado. Chaco Culture National Historical Park, located north and west of Albuquerque, contains eighteen square miles of ruins, including major and minor building sites and miles of straight ceremonial ways or roads. The Chacoans built great houses, such as those of Pueblo Bonito. These were multi-terraced room blocks containing up to 700 rooms and many

kivas, some of them great kivas that could hold hundreds of people at a time for ceremonies. Other ruins at Chaco Canyon include Chetro Ketl, Casa Rinconada, and Pueblo del Arroyo.

The Pueblos believe that it was the ancestors of the Keresans (a contemporary language group) who lived in Chaco Canyon. It was the center of the Ancient Ones' culture from about A.D. 900 to 1150. Thousands of people could have lived there,

though it is probable that the people inhabited the city at capacity only seasonally. The arts were well developed and included fine pottery, weaving, basketry, and jewelry of stone (especially turquoise), shell, and bone. After periods of drought, Chaco Canyon was finally abandoned.

Mesa Verde National Park in southwestern Colorado contains more than 4,000 sites, ranging from pithouse ruins to elaborate pueblos built inside huge caves, high in the cliffs.

Within the Canyon de Chelly National Monument, in northwestern Arizona, are more than 700 sites, including the famed White House

Ruin, Canyon del Muerto, Mummy Cave, and Antelope House, as well as pithouse remains. The 130 square miles of Canyon de Chelly are today owned by the Navajo, who began to settle there around 1700.

Other Ancient Ones inhabited villages in what is now Bandelier National Monument, near Los Alamos, New Mexico, from about A.D. 500 to the late 1500s. The ruins show various types of buildings, ranging from rooms dug out of the soft canyon walls to cliff-hung rooms to a large pueblo built in the open that contained as many as 400 rooms.

Top: Canyon de Chelly
Right: Bandelier

Acoma

Lucy Lewis

Conroy Chino

Concepción Faustine

Indian name: *Ako-meó: "People of the White Rock"*

Language: *Keres*

Feast Day: *September 2*

Location: *On a mesa 65 miles west of Albuquerque.*

Area: *248,000 acres*   Population: *3,676*

Joseph Cerna

Acoma ladders

Acoma's thousand-year-old "sky city" is famous the world over for its romantic evocation of the Pueblo past when many villages were built atop the steep mesas of the Southwest. The mesa tops, difficult to climb and relatively easy to defend, were ideal locations for defensive purposes, though most often dry and far from cultivated fields.

When Francisco Vasquez de Coronado's men arrived at Acoma in 1540, they met with natives who came down the cliffs to greet them, but the Spanish made no attempt to scale the rock. In 1598, Juan de Oñate visited the Pueblo and its several thousand inhabitants without incident. However, later that year his nephew led a force up to Acoma and became embroiled in a battle that led to his defeat and death, as well as to the deaths of many Spaniards, either at the hands of Natives or by falling over the cliffs.

Oñate sent a punitive expedition in 1599 led by the brother of the dead nephew. In the battle that followed, the Pueblo was destroyed, hundreds of Acoma's residents were killed and five hundred were captured. The captives were punished viciously; all men over the age of twenty-five had one foot cut off and were subjected to twenty years of slavery. Women and younger men were also condemned to twenty years of slavery, and the captive children were sent away to be missionized by priests.

No priests arrived in Acoma until 1629, when the San Estevan mission was erected, and when the village itself was substantially rebuilt; some of these structures are still standing. The priest assigned to the Mission at Acoma was killed during the Pueblo Revolt, but otherwise Acoma did not participate in the revolt. The depredations of disease and drought also played a role in reducing the population, so that by 1900 less than five hundred people remained in the sky city that had once been so populous.

Perhaps the mesa top was always too far from food and water sources; in any case, modern life is not conducive to climbing a 400-foot cliff every day on the way to and from work. Today most Acoma Pueblo people live in towns below the mesa and derive their income from tourism, the cattle business, and a casino. The casino revenue is being used for long-needed improvements to Acoma's outdated and inadequate water system.

Concepción Faustine

Selling pottery

Joseph & Barbara Cerna

Lucy Lewis & daughters

Only a few families live in the sky city today, but all Acoma Natives feel a strong connection to this lofty Pueblo, and the village and mission on top of the mesa are lovingly maintained.

Acoma is known for a thin-walled pottery made from an especially tough gray clay. The clay is so difficult to work, however, that some modern Acoma artists are turning to clay from other pueblos for their pots, which they decorate with traditional Acoma designs, such as delicate cross-hatching, or animals and flowers. Both the style of pottery and its decoration were influenced by Mimbres traditions. Lucy Lewis is a celebrated Acoma potter. The potters of Acoma sometimes portray parrots on their pottery. In the time of the Ancient Ones, parrots were traded to Chaco Canyon from Mexico and seem to have been important for their feathers.

Acoma cemetery

Acoma Pueblo people are organized into clans according to the mother's membership. A traditional Acoma Native would only marry outside the clan. The Pueblo leader is a cacique, who is both spiritual head and chief official. The governors are chosen from among the Antelope Clan.

Village scene

Acoma church

Many Acoma people honor both Christian and indigenous spiritual beliefs, and this colorful marriage of cultures is visible on San Estevan Feast Day, annually celebrated on September 2. The image of the saint (Saint Stephen) is carried from the mission church and placed in the plaza, where dances are performed before it. The Green Corn dance begins the festivities, and may be followed by Deer or Eagle dances. At the conclusion of the day the image is restored to its place inside the church.

Remembering the ancestors

Acoma pottery

Conroy Chino

Conroy Chino from Acoma is a well-known television investigative reporter. He says, "It will always be the place I call home, no matter where I go in my job as a television reporter. It will always be a very sacred and spiritual place for me. It is a place that will always bring fond memories of my childhood and is a reminder of who I am. It is at the heart of my people's spiritual belief system. I frequently go back there for the rituals and ceremonies, because it is so sacred."

There is a visitor center and museum near the foot of the mesa, from where van tours to the Pueblo atop the mesa are available.

The old and the new

There in the west
   Is the home of the rain gods,
There in the west
   is their water pool,
In the middle of the water pool
   is the spruce tree
   that they use as a ladder,
Up from the water the rain gods
   draw the crops which give us life,
East from there, on the place
   where we dance, they lay the crops,
Then up from that place the people
   receive crops and life.

           — Acoma Prayer

Acoma pot
Next pages: Acoma water pool

Lucy Lewis

35

Cochiti

Regis Pecos

Mary Sadie Benevidez

Mary Trujillo

Arnold Herrera

Indian Name: Katyete, or Ko-chits: "Stone Kiva"

Language: Keres

Feast Day: July 14

Location: 47 miles north of Albuquerque, by Cochiti Lake.

Area: 53,779 acres   Population: 1,050

Cochiti Lake

Cochiti Pueblo people, like most Keresan speakers, trace their ancestry back to a mystical "white house," believed to be located at Chaco Canyon, where they lived before arriving on the west side of the Rio Grande. Archaeological evidence suggests that their ancestors moved into the area in the twelfth century, and that Cochiti village itself may date from about A.D. 1225, making it among the oldest of the pueblos.

Of all of the pueblos, Cochiti has been one of the most strongly influenced by Spanish culture. Its mission church, with its heavy beams and wooden balcony, has a prominent role in the village, and the Pueblo buildings, tinted pink and yellow, suggest a Latin influence not seen at other earth-brown pueblos. Cochiti relations with the Spanish have gone through distinct highs and lows since the first encounters in the sixteenth century.

Initial visits from the Spanish were cordially received, but as the Spanish began to exact their demands for tribute and service and to punish capriciously those who resisted, the Cochiti people increased their resistance. They joined their neighbors in the Pueblo Revolt of 1680. After the revolt, some people from Cochiti who had fled their Pueblo helped to found Laguna Pueblo, while others withdrew to nearby Horn Mesa on the Pajarito Plateau and built a village there. In 1696, after the Spanish reconquest, Diego de Vargas, aided by friendly Natives, led his troops to the top of the mesa and destroyed that village. Eventually the remaining Cochiti people moved back to the original Pueblo.

Originally, the Cochiti were farmers, though they always required irrigation to supplement the irregular rainfall. Even today, says Cochiti resident Regis Pecos, "90 percent of the available agricultural land is still under cultivation." Many Cochiti people work off the reservation, particularly at Los Alamos and Santa Fe, and some pursue traditional crafts, such as pottery and beadwork.

The men of Cochiti Pueblo make especially fine large drums from hollowed cottonwood covered with hide, which they sometimes paint and decorate. Drummers throughout all the pueblos use drums such as those made at Cochiti to sound the beat of the sacred dances.

A familiar form of clay sculpture at Cochiti Pueblo is the storyteller, a seated figure in the act of telling a story, often with eyes closed and mouth open. Smaller figures swarm over the

storyteller, listening, playing, enrapt in the adult's act of recall. The storyteller may be human or animal; frogs and bears are popular storytellers. Helen Cordero, a Pueblo artist, created the storytellers in the 1960s, and they have subsequently become much emulated among other artists, both Cochiti and non-Cochiti. Today storytellers are a collectors' item, popular among those who appreciate Native American arts.

San Buenaventura's Feast Day, observed at Cochiti Pueblo on July 14, offers a colorful festival with dances that are open to the public. Though the church is a center of village activity, the two kiva groups, the Squash People and the Turquoise People, respectively, use the two round kivas for their ceremonies. A single cacique serves as religious leader of the Pueblo.

Left: Gabriel Trujillo and Dawn

Leon Ortiz and son Kyle

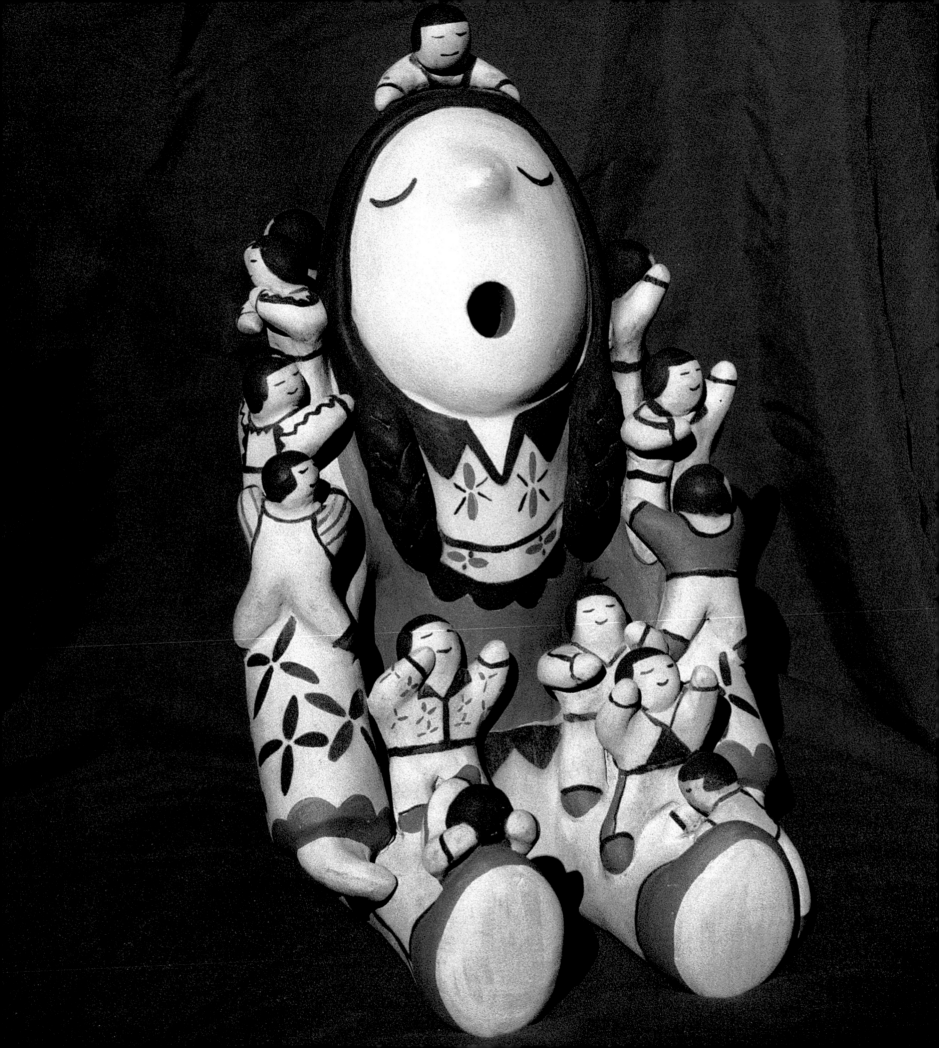

Of Cochiti's government system, Regis Pecos says, "It is theocratic; there is no separation of 'church and state.' Religious leaders call to service individuals who are able to lead by example. Individuals with a command of the language, the traditions, and the culture are called to serve their people and to sustain the vitality of the community. This is one of the highest and most noble callings imaginable."

In the 1970s, the building of Cochiti Dam created a reservoir above the village. Around the shores of Cochiti Lake, as the reservoir is known, the Pueblo has leased land to a developer, who

Left: Storyteller by Mary & Leonard Trujillo   Below: April Trujillo & her storyteller

Trisha Moquino and her mother, Abby

erected a modern shopping center and a retirement center with recreational facilities. Boat ramps and campsites line the lake, creating an atmosphere of modernity that has impacted the rest of the Pueblo, which today has electricity and running water.

NA ORTIZ

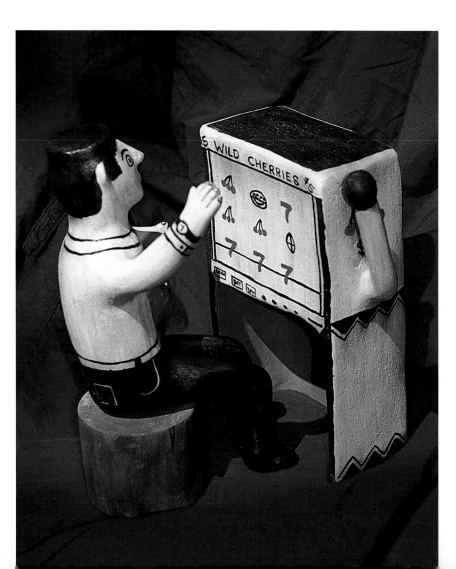

Clockwise from top left:

Storytellers by Seferina Ortiz
in her home

Seferina Ortiz

"United We Drum" by Mary Trujillo

Mary Trujillo with
her granddaughter, Dawn

Gambling figurine by Joyce Ortiz

Deer dancers and storyteller by
Mary Trujillo

47

Isleta

August Shattuck

Sophie Salvador

Luther Joyala

Agnes Dill

Indian Name: Shiewhibak: "Knife Laid on the Ground to Play Whib"

Language: Southern Tiwa

Feast Day: September 4

Location: 22 miles south of Albuquerque

Area: 211,002 acres   Population: 3,401

Isleta has always been fertile, and its riverside location made it prosperous from its beginnings around the fourteenth century. Perhaps in the past the nearby Rio Grande did occasionally swirl around the hilltop town, turning it into the "little island" for which the Spanish named it San Antonio de la Isleta. The Indian name, "knife laid on the ground to play whib," may refer to the sharp lava ridge of the mountain beyond. Whib is a native footrace that resembles a relay race.

In 1675, surviving Natives from the Salinas culture area east of the Rio Grande Valley moved into the Isleta Pueblo region, and some of them may have been among the ancestors of the present-day Isleta people.

When the Spanish first arrived, Isleta was one of a dozen or so Tiwa-speaking villages along the Rio Grande. In 1581 two explorers leading a group of Spaniards were offered food by the welcoming Isletans. By the time of the 1680 Pueblo Revolt, even if the Isleta people had wanted to join, it is doubtful that they could have, since the Pueblo was occupied with Spanish troops and later filled up with Spanish refugees. Instead, the Isletans fled to the hills.

The following year, Governor Antonio Otermìn attempted to bring the pueblos under Spanish control again. He marched up the Rio Grande to Isleta and, apparently enraged that its mission church had been partly destroyed, attacked the Pueblo and burned it to the ground, taking 519 captives. After the reconquest, the Spanish were able to persuade some of the Isleta people to return to the Pueblo and rebuild.

Isleta Pueblo people are divided into two groups: Red Eye People and Black Eye People. The rectangular kiva of the Red Eye People is built into the northernmost house block, and that of the Black Eye People stands by itself in the southern part of the Pueblo. All members belong to one of seven corn groups, who are led by the Corn Mother or the Corn Father.

Agnes Dill, of Isleta Pueblo, has described the centrality of corn to the Pueblo belief system: "There are six colors of corn: yellow, white, blue, black, red, and speckled. And each color stands for a direction: north, south, east and west, up and down. The solid colors are for the four main directions. White is for the east, where the sun

Agnes Dill

rises, and blue is for the west. Yellow is for the north and red is for the south."

Traditionally, the day begins and ends with prayers. "Early in the morning, my mother would wake me up and say, before sunup, 'Go distant and say a prayer,'" Agnes Dill remembers. "I'd take white cornmeal, already ground, and pray for myself and for my home, always to the east. Then at noontime, when I would come back from herding sheep, I would take corn pollen and I'd go distant and say a prayer again. And then in the evening before the sun was down, I'd go distant and use yellow cornmeal and would pray again. I would pray every day."

The ritual functions are directed by the war chief. The governor, president, vice-president, and a council are elected.

The large round building in the southern part of the Pueblo belongs to all of the people rather than to a single secret society. Said to be the oldest structure in the Pueblo, it is used for dances.

The stairs that lead to the entrance have replaced the ladder that formerly stood there. The ladder was a reminder of the mythical ladder by which the Isleta people climbed from their former world into this one.

Children playing ball

Isleta street scene

The Pueblo derives major income from a casino, golf course, and gas station. Pueblo people are very community-oriented, and profits from the collective businesses run by Isleta Pueblo are committed to projects that benefit the entire community. Casino revenue contributes to a supervised youth center for recreation and other activities, as well as a drug and alcohol rehabilitation center, serving the surrounding communities.

Luther Joyala

Isleta Gaming Palace

56

Tonita Abeyta

Jemez

Roger Madalena

Guadalupe Chosa

Anna Marie Pecos

Estella Loretto

Indian Name: Wala-towa: "People in the Canyon"

Language: Towa

Feast Day: November 12

Location: On Jemez Creek, 30 miles northwest of Bernalillo

Area: 89,624 acres   Population: 2,378

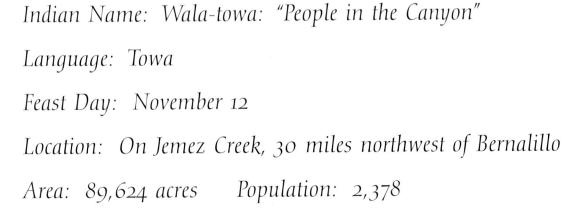

Christmas altar

Joe S. Sando

Jemez, the only Towa-speaking pueblo, was probably founded sometime in the early 1600s. The Spanish, visiting in 1541, reported seven pueblos, some along the Jemez Creek and some located atop nearby mesas, probably for defensive purposes. At the time, Spanish practice was to urge Natives in scattered villages to consolidate, the better to control and missionize them, and the present-day Jemez Pueblo grew up as a result of this policy.

Jemez oral tradition and archaeology both point to the possibility that the ancestors of the Jemez lived at Sand Canyon Pueblo west of Cortez, Colorado, and gradually moved to the present location. The name "Jemez" is derived from the Towa word "hemish," meaning "people."

The history of Jemez-Spanish relations is a tale of resistance and reprisals. In one famous event of the mid-seventeenth century, twenty-nine Jemez men were hanged in retribution for the death of one Spaniard. In 1680, Jemez people participated in the Pueblo Revolt and afterward retreated to the mesa tops or fled to Navajo and Hopi country. The Jemez who remained in New Mexico fought the Spanish with vigor when they returned in the reconquest, but suffered a brutal defeat in 1694 in which three hundred and sixty-one women and children were captured and eighty-four Jemez were killed. The Jemez people's food stores and livestock were carried off, leaving the survivors destitute. Various revolts and rebellions continued for two more years, until the Spanish were able, in 1696, to pacify the remaining scattered, impoverished, and war-weary Pueblo people.

Jemez historian Joe Sando has described the religious repression visited upon the pueblos by both the Spanish and the Americans: Under the Spanish, "religious doctrine and observances were rigidly and harshly suppressed. . . . Disobedience was punished. . . . Homes were raided for religious paraphernalia . . . and punishment meted out to the offenders." Two hundred years later, the indigenous people were faced with similar horrors at the hands of "God-fearing" Anglos. Among the destructive acts of the American government was the imposition of the Religious Crimes Code, under which almost all Pueblo religious observances and gatherings were banned.

By the early nineteenth century, the population of Jemez was much depleted. It was given a size-able boost when Pecos Pueblo was abandoned in 1838 due to warfare and disease, and the few Pecos survivors were invited to move in with their Jemez neighbors. The two groups merged their traditions and history.

Jemez Pueblo people follow a traditional way of life, farming and making pottery and woven goods. They are particularly noted for their baskets, which are made from yucca fibers, as well as for woven cotton belts and headbands. Footraces are another Jemez tradition, and the Pueblo's young men are world-renowned runners

Lupe and Guadalupe Chosa

who have set records for running to mountain-tops in New Mexico and Colorado.

The two large rectangular kivas that dominate the plaza belong to the Turquoise and Squash groups into which the Pueblo is traditionally divided. Jemez also has a clan system and a single cacique who serves for life. Feast day dances in August and in November honor, respectively, Our Lady of the Angels for the Pecos descendants and San Diego for the Jemez. Jemez dances are widely attended; crowds are attracted by the colorfully costumed dancers accompanied by a large chorus. Says Carlotta Toya of Jemez, "All our dances are meaningful because they are prayers for all people. Even if we don't know them, we pray for them. We pray for everybody when we dance."

Visitors can view the Jemez ruins dating from A.D. 1250 and the ruins of a Spanish mission from the 1620s in a self-guided tour of Jemez State Monument, twelve miles north of the Pueblo.

Isadore Chinana

Carnel Chosa returned to Jemez Pueblo after graduating from college and is now a policy and legislative analyst for the New Mexico Office of Indian Affairs. He says, "After graduating from Dartmouth and receiving my Masters from Harvard, I returned to my home, because I wanted to be near my family, and also because I feel that my education and experience being away combined with my traditional Pueblo culture has given me a better opportunity to help my people. I also returned so that I can assist and be a resource for Indian kids who want to go away and come home as I have done."

Isadore Chinana and family

Florence Shewiwi and her brother, Guadalupe Chosa

Carnel Chosa

64

Each Christmas, a different family is given the honor of providing a "home" for the Holy Family from December 24 to January 6. Statues are brought from the church, and a manger is created for them. Everyone in the Pueblo comes to celebrate and to enjoy a feast.

Pauline T. Correo at the Toledo home

Estella Loretto and her sculpture

Estella Loretto, who is a sculptor and owner of Gentle Spirit Gallery, says of her art, "I would like to create pieces that speak for positive environmental change through art. I believe that we have the opportunity as Native people to impact the global human family by subliminally conveying the sacred messages from the ancient teachings of our people."

Lucy Lowden's Little People

Joe and Lucy Lowden

Juana Marie Pecos holding statue of the Blessed Katari Takawitha

Roger Madalena, member of New Mexico House of Representatives

Laguna

John Alonza

Suzie Rayos Marmon

Johnnie Wardlow

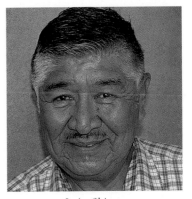

Irvin Shiosee

Indian Name: Ka-waikah: "Lake People"

Language: Keres

Feast Days: March 19 & September 19

Location: 47 miles west of Albuquerque

Area: 415,910 acres   Population: 6,233

Eagle Dance

Laguna, one of the most populous pueblos, is stretched out over six villages, including Old Laguna. Laguna's governance unifies the Pueblo both traditionally and secularly. There are three main villages: Old Laguna, Paguate, and Mesita, with Old Laguna being the capital. The other villages are Paraje, Searma, and Encinal. Each village, with its own different customs and ceremonial days, tends to go its own way. This wide variation in style and expression is the result of Laguna's history.

The Pueblo was populated by refugees from the Rio Grande area in 1694. They came from the permanently abandoned village of La Cienega, and from Cochiti, Santo Domingo, and Jemez. The Acomas had allowed them to settle on the mesa north of Acoma, but Spanish Governor Pedro Rodriguez Cubero persuaded the refugees to leave the mesa and return home. They stayed to rest at a large lake (laguna) and received permission to settle there on July 2, 1698. The church of San José de Laguna was completed by 1699. Although the lake no longer exists, Laguna Pueblo remains.

The village of Old Laguna has the most famous historic site on the Pueblo—the stunningly white adobe mission church of San José completed in 1699. Inside the heavy wooden doors is a beautifully painted interior that is cool on the hottest of days. The paintings combine traditional Catholic themes with Native symbols and designs, in an intercultural celebration of belief. Old Laguna holds a celebration annually on the Feast Day of San José, March 19, as well as a fall feast day on September 19.

Since 1889 the Santa Fe Railroad has come through the reservation, and Laguna men employed by the railroad moved their families to other places along the railroad line. Today Laguna people make their living both in traditional crafts like pottery and in high-tech businesses on and off the reservation. A uranium mine on Laguna land once provided much income to the Pueblo. The most successful business of all, however, is Laguna Industries, a company that has earned millions in government contracts and private subcontracts for products that include communications shelter units that were used during the Persian Gulf War.

Preparing for feast

Irvin W. Shiosee, of Laguna, describing the Pueblo blend of tradition and modernity, quotes his adored grandfather, a cattle and sheep rancher who lived to be 127 years old: "He used to say, 'You can build a bridge, but don't expect everyone to cross it. Some will have to remain where they are, while others will walk on over.' What he meant was 'don't try to bring all your people from the old to the new customs, because not everybody will follow you.' Some will follow, but others like life the way it is."

Yvonne and Irvin Shiosee with grandson

Suzie Rayos Marmon

Izzie Sarracino with her daughter Johnnie Wardlow

Izzie Sarracino enjoys preparing for feast days. She says, "I cook all the traditional foods—chile, posole, Indian bread, and bread pudding. Seeing my family and friends enjoy my food gives me joy. The Creator has given me this food so that I may share it and that my family and friends may grow healthy from eating it."

*Morning
procession*

*Next pages:
Old Laguna*

Feast day procession

Nambé

Gil Peña

Cloud Eagle

Brian Peña

Indian Name: Nambé or Nambi: "Mound of Earth in the Corner,"

or "People of the Round Earth"

Language: Tewa

Feast Day: October 4

Location: About 17 miles northeast of Santa Fe

Area: 19,076 acres   Population: 438

Claudine Peña Abeyta

Nambé, inhabited since around A.D. 1300, is one of the most scenic of pueblos, located below the Sangre de Cristo Mountains and near Nambé Falls. The falls are sacred to the Nambé people and the site of a spectacular July 4 celebration and dance. Brian Peña, a ranger there, says, "Nambé Falls was where the old Pueblo was located; the ruins are still there. As a ranger, I try to protect them from vandals. We feel it means a lot to our culture and beliefs to keep the dwellings of our forefathers sacrosanct."

For centuries, Nambé was a prosperous community of farmers and hunters, whose fields, watered by the river, produced corn, squash, and beans. Sixteenth-century Spanish visitors told of Nambé families who each had two or three rooms full of stored corn. This surplus, of course, was very attractive to the Spanish, who abused the Natives' generosity with their demands for food and service when they settled in the area. The Nambé Pueblo people participated in the Pueblo Revolt in 1680. In 1696 they battled again, unsuccessfully, to throw off Spanish control, but afterward submitted and gradually became relatively Hispanicized over the ensuing centuries.

Like neighboring Pojoaque, the Nambé people dwindled due to disease until the population was greatly reduced. By the middle of the twentieth century, Nambé rarely observed its traditional ceremonials and few of its inhabitants could speak Tewa. Among those who could, however, was Moses Peña, the governor for many terms. Moses Peña undertook to teach the old stories and religious traditions to the younger generations, helping them, in the process, to retain and pass on their Tewa language. A renaissance in traditional observances followed, and today the Pueblo has become reinvigorated, in terms of both population and culture. It is revitalizing its traditional arts and crafts, including the making of micaceous pottery, weaving, and beadwork. Nambé Pueblo has been registered as a National Historic Landmark.

Gilbert Peña has served seven times as the Pueblo's governor and is Dean of Students of the Santa Fe Indian School. "When my uncle, Moses Peña, went to this school," Gil Peña says, "Indian languages and customs were forbidden. Today the nineteen pueblos own and operate the school. The curriculum is as modern as in any American school, but it includes Indian issues and culture,

and the school schedule lets students participate
in their traditional ceremonies and feast days."

There is a single, circular kiva at Nambé.
According to Tewa custom, the people are divided
into two groups, each with their own cacique. The
Summer cacique is in charge of the South People
and the Winter cacique the North People.

Preparing for the Eagle Dance

Gil Peña

Says Gil Peña, "For so many years, Pueblo people have survived because, in my opinion, the teachings of our elders have been so cherished and honored. As we enter the next century, my concern is the survival of our culture and tradition. Our children need to absorb what is given to us by our past."

His daughter Claudine Peña Abeyta, an electronic technician in Los Alamos, agrees. "My father has taught me to value my tradition and culture. I've learned to balance that with my work and education. I think it is a very valuable way of life, and now I'm learning to bring up my three-year-old son Robert with that foundation."

"The wisdom and advice that is passed on is the very breath and spirit of who we are as a people," Gil Peña concludes.

Claudine Peña Abeyta with her son Robert

Ernest Mirabal Jr. (Cloud Eagle)

Shield dance

Deer Dancers on kiva steps

Picuris

Gerald Nailor

Connie Tsosie Gaussoin

Juan José Martinez

Wayne Nez Gaussoin

Indian Name: Pikuri: "Those Who Paint"

Language: Northern Tiwa

Feast Day: August 10

Location: Sangre de Cristo Mountains, between Santa Fe & Taos

Area: 14,947 acres   Population: 245

Hidden Valley is an appropriate name for the site of Picuris Pueblo, occupied as early as A.D. 900. This Pueblo was so well concealed that the first Spanish explorer to the Southwest, Francisco Vasquez de Coronado, missed it entirely when he came through in 1540. It was not until nearly the end of the sixteenth century, in 1591, that another Spaniard, Castaño de Sosa, finally made it to the remote village. At the time it must have seemed an imposing place; Castaño de Sosa reported that the Pueblo was seven to nine stories high. Certainly there were more inhabitants at Picuris then than the 300 or so who dwell there today.

The remote location of Picuris Pueblo spared it some of the worst harassment by the Spanish and delayed encroachment by other European settlers. But Picuris and Taos have long been linked by culture and proximity, and many of the Picuris men played a leading role in the Pueblo Revolt of 1680. The years that followed saw repeated efforts by the Picuris people to resist or evade the burdens and repression imposed by the Spanish, and many people left the Pueblo to live for a time among the Apaches at Quarto Lejo.

No enemy of the Picuris has been as powerful as disease; the Pueblo suffered so from various epidemics that for a time it was completely abandoned. In recent years, however, the population has begun to rebound, along with a renewed interest in traditional culture.

One can see the remains of the massive pueblo of the era of Coronado and Castaño de Sosa on a hill to the north of the present village. The most conspicuous sight is the "tower," the remains of a round, above-ground kiva.

Today the population at Picuris is on the rise, and the fields below the village are cultivated with corn, beans, and squash, though most of the Pueblo's people make their living by working outside the reservation. In an unusual business arrangement, the people of Picuris, in partnership with a developer, currently run a luxury hotel, the Hotel Santa Fe. The hotel provides revenue and jobs for the tribe.

The chief craft specialty of the village is an undecorated pottery made with micaceous clay. The sparkling specks of mica in the clay are not just ornamental; they temper it so that it is watertight and heat-resistant and therefore useful for cooking.

Another craft, jewelry making, is represented by Connie Tsosie Gaussoin, who draws strength from her traditional roots. She writes: "By soldering, hammering metal, or carving into tufa, a feeling of spiritual blessings surrounds me, which offers me strength and harmony within myself as an artist."

Connie Tsosie Gaussoin with her son, Wayne Nez Gaussoin

Cora L. Durand

Picuris also has some famous painters and potters. A former governor, Gerald Nailor, is a well known artist. Anthony Duran follows the family tradition with his pottery, and. Lonnie Vigil is a well known potter.

Corn Dances are held in June and August, and the Pueblo's feast day, the Feast of San Lorenzo on August 12, features dances and footraces. There is a restaurant and museum showing the ancient ruins and artifacts.

Anthony Durand with his micaceous pot

Gerald Nailor, artist & former governor

Shane & Rebecca Shemayme doing Belt Dance at Hotel Santa Fe

San Lorenzo Church

Baking bread in horno

Round house & ancient ruins

Recreation of kiva in Picuris museum

Pojoaque

Governor Jake Viarrial

Lt. Governor George Rivera

Charlie Tapia

Crucita Tapia

Indian Name: P'o Suwae Geh: "Place to Drink Water"

Language: Tewa

Feast Day: December 12

Location: 15 miles north of Santa Fe

Area: 11,601 acres   Population: 240

Buffalo dancers entering kiva

Pojoaque has the smallest population of all the pueblos in New Mexico. It is currently occupied by about one hundred people. The village is growing rather than dwindling, however, returning from near-extinction near the beginning of the twentieth century.

When the Spaniards first saw Pojoaque, it was one of eighty Indian pueblos in the Rio Grande Valley. Most of these villages have vanished today and Pojoaque nearly met the same fate, due to warfare and disease, particularly a smallpox epidemic in 1890. The people apparently abandoned their Pueblo by 1915, and Anglo and Hispanic farmers subsequently occupied much of their lands. It is probable that the few remaining Pojoaque families were living in nearby towns such as Santa Fe and only returning occasionally to check on their ancestral properties. One of the last residents, a rain priest named Antonio Tapia, donated his sacred water vials to the Museum of New Mexico, thinking they would never be used again.

Fortunately, Pojoaque's land claims were clearly established. In 1863, Abraham Lincoln had presented the Pueblo leader with a cane of office of the type received by all Pueblo leaders. This cane was inscribed "A. Lincoln," and was similar to canes previously presented to the Pueblo caciques by the King of Spain and the Mexican government. Though the cane was lost, Pojoaque received a new Spanish cane in 1998. Today all Pueblo people treasure these canes as symbols of authority and hand them down from leader to leader.

More important from a legal point of view, the United States had in 1864 patented the Spanish land grant to Pojoaque Pueblo, an act that gave the reservation legal status. Based on the legitimacy of this land grant, in 1933 some of its land was restored to descendants of the original population, forty of whom were located in the area. Pojoaque descendants moved back to the village and revitalized the Pueblo.

Among those who returned was Charles Tapia, a grandson of the last rain priest. Charles Tapia was born in Texas but was brought back to Pojoaque as an infant. "When I was a boy," Tapia remembers, "Pojoaque had 20 people and five houses. Now there are between 240 and 260 people." As an adult, Tapia joined the Air Force, served in Viet Nam, and returned to Pojoaque permanently in 1973, becoming war chief in 1992. "It is a great honor for me to be war chief," he says. "I have four war captains to help me take care of the kiva and the tribal activities."

The people of Pojoaque have worked hard to restore their traditions, and Tapia has been an enthusiastic advocate of repatriation, negotiating for the return of his ancestors' bones, and persuading the Museum of New Mexico to return his grandfather's sacred water vials.

Today, the residents of Pojoaque earn their living through traditional crafts and modern businesses. One of the newest endeavors is the thriving Cities of Gold Casino, named for the mythical cities the Spanish were seeking when they first encountered the Pueblo people. Cities of Gold is one of the largest casinos in the state. Profits from the casino have paid for improvements such as a new kiva and a day care center for the elders who need companionship. In addition, Pojoaque has a hotel and shopping center, and the Pueblo leases land to businesses along the highway. Its people make distinguished pottery, needlework, and beadwork. Collectors particularly prize the pottery of Lucy Year Flower.

Cities of Gold Casino

Pojoaque's Poeh Center and Museum offers training and experience in traditional arts and crafts to Native Americans throughout New Mexico, teaching basketweaving, pottery, embroidery, drummaking, and sculpture. The program is partly funded by the profits from Cities of Gold Casino, and is considered by the U. S. Department of Education to be one of the most successful in the country.

The traditional cacique system was abolished when the town was depopulated, and after the Pueblo was restored, its people began to elect the governor and tribal council.

The mission church in Pojoaque Pueblo, dedicated to Our Lady of Guadalupe, dates from 1706. On December 12, her feast day is celebrated with Bow Dances and a Buffalo Dance, attended by many Pueblo people and visitors.

Lieutenant Governor George Rivera says, "No matter what it is we do, whether it is to dance, or create art, or demonstrate how we handle business relations, we need to believe strongly in ourselves, to be confident in what we do so our people will have confidence, too."

Governor Jake Viarrial

Lt. Governor George Rivera in his studio

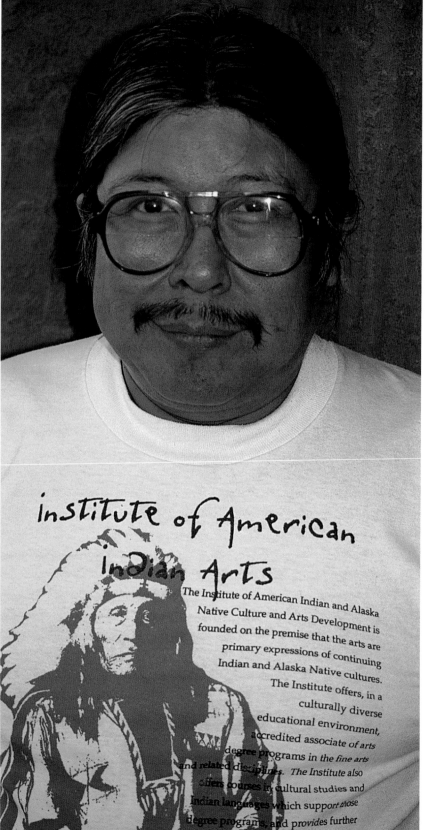

Charlie Tapia

Buffalo Dance

Ester Tapia

Entering kiva

Lt. Governor George Rivera with his sculpture

Pojoaque Pueblo
Poeh Cultural Center

Sandia

Lynn Trujillo

Bertha Lente

Victoria Whipple

Indian Name: Na-fiat: "Sandy" or "Dusty"

Language: Southern Tiwa

Feast Day: June 13

Location: 13 miles north of Albuquerque

Area: 22,884 acres   Population: 318

Christina Otero

San Antonio Church

Sandia is one of a dozen pueblos, called the Province of Tiguex by the Spanish, that existed along the Rio Grande in the sixteenth century from Isleta Pueblo north to the present town of Bernalillo. Spanish explorers called the pueblo Sandia, Spanish for "watermelon," apparently because of melon patches at the Pueblo, and the name was subsequently applied to the mountain range just to the east.

Today only two pueblos remain of the Southern Tiwa group encountered by the Spanish in 1540, when the Vasquez de Coronado expedition arrived and set about spending its first winter among these villages. The Spanish had expected to feed and clothe the 1,200 men and 559 horses in their party by confiscating food and blankets from the Natives. Their excessive demands and the Natives' resulting suspicion and hostility led to open confrontation, particularly at a village called Arenal. There a party of Pueblo people, enraged over the demands and further incensed by an alleged rape, stole a number of horses and killed them. Coronado ordered Arenal to be attacked in reprisal. The village was completely destroyed and its residents slaughtered;

some were burned at the stake. Many of the details of history suggest that Arenal was inhabited by Tiwas.

Sandia Pueblo did not have recorded contact with the Spanish until the end of the sixteenth century, when a missionary friar arrived. During the next hundred years, the dozen Southern Tiwa pueblos were consolidated into four, including Isleta and Sandia. The Sandia people joined in the Pueblo Revolt in 1680, burning their own church and abandoning the village. The Spanish retaliated by burning the village twice more. The Sandias scattered all over, but a large group of them went west to live among the Hopis, where they stayed until 1742. By the time they returned to their homeland, only Isleta and Sandia remained of the twelve Southern Tiwa towns first seen by the Spanish.

In the nineteenth century, Hispanic farms and ranches all around the Sandia reservation began to influence the Pueblo culture, and the proximity of Albuquerque has brought modernization into the lives of the Sandia people.

Sandia Casino

According to tradition, the Pueblo is divided into two groups—the Turquoise People and the Squash People, and further subdivided into corn groups and matrilineal clans. A cacique serves for life; under him is a war chief, who also serves for life. The feast day dances honor Saint Anthony on June 13.

Sandia Pueblo operates a modern gaming facility that has brought many jobs home to its Pueblo. From the profits, it has built a recreational center, a senior citizens building, and a Head Start school. The trading post and lake recreation also add to the Pueblo's income.

Buffalos were purchased with casino money

Sandia's Early Childhood Program recognizes that children's "work" is really to play. As Early Childhood teacher, Debi Kruse, says, "When children are engaged in play, they are learning all the necessary skills to become independent, productive adults." In a nurturing environment, the program addresses all aspects of children's development, including thinking abilities, physical activity, social interaction, and play skills. The well-trained staff is a resource for the community as a whole.

Cristina Otero, Sandia Pueblo Educational Coordinator, describes recent developments in education in the Pueblo: "In 1996 the Tribal Council increased education assistance, approving a program to fund students to attend the higher learning institution of their choice, regardless of cost or location, as well as a Higher Education Grant through the Bureau of Indian Affairs. The Tribal Scholarship program covers needs not met through other programs. The Tribal Council also approved a College Preparatory/Private School Scholarship program that will fund students ages 18 months through 12th grade. Thirty-six Sandia students—approximately one-third of all Sandia students—are enrolled under this program."

*Larissa Bernal slides down with
Deon Montoya looking on*

New housing project built with money from casino

Doctor Gloyd checking eyes of José Trujillo in Health Center

Wellness Program Coordinator Paul Hepfer describes the work of the Pueblo Outdoor Experience and Wellness Programs: "The outdoor challenge program incorporates challenge and perceived risk to provide powerful experiences. Wellness programs include a wide variety of activities to address nutrition, physical health and mental well-being for children, families, and senior citizens within the community. Exercise programs are available with a physician's referral."

Staff meeting in new Tribal Council chambers

Sandia Lake

Lynn Trujillo graduated from Dartmouth and is now in her second year of law school and working for an Albuquerque law firm. She reflects on her Sandia Pueblo upbringing: "I realized when I went east to school, how important my home and my family culture were to me, and how they were able to keep me grounded. I truly feel that no matter where I am or what I'm doing, I will never forget who I am and where I came from. My father encouraged me to go off and wasn't worried that I wouldn't come back. I went to school with tribal scholarships that came from gaming. I will always come home and participate in the ceremonies. We have so many more options now, and having this future will help me help my people."

San Felipe

Frank Tenorio

Sara Candelaria

Darrell Candelaria

Jennifer Garcia Calabaza

Indian Name: Koots-cha

Language: Keres

Feast Day: May 1

Location: 29 miles north of Albuquerque

Area: 48,930 acres   Population: 2,326

San Felipe Pueblo was once on the main road, the Camino Real, or Royal Road, which led to Mexico City. But today this pueblo by the Rio Grande is distinctly off the beaten track. By its own choice, it is possibly one of the most conservative of the Keresan-speaking pueblos.

The San Felipe community is very much focused on maintaining ancient Pueblo customs and beliefs through proper conduct, religious training and ceremonies, and through an emphasis on communal, rather than individual, social values. The community is divided into two groups for ceremonial purposes: the Squash or Pumpkin Group and the Turquoise Group. Two round kivas on the Pueblo provide shelter for the most sacred activities of these groups. A single cacique serves as religious leader.

The exception to San Felipe's atmosphere of quiet remove occurs on feast days, when it throws open its doors with a burst of hospitality. The Pueblo has an ideal "stage" in its plaza, where a deep depression, worn down through centuries of dancing feet, creates a kind of natural amphitheater. The Green Corn Dances performed here on May 1 to the accompaniment of resounding drums and a male chorus are very colorful and widely attended. The missionizing Spanish assigned each pueblo a saint, and assigned St. Philip, or San Felipe, to this pueblo.

Though farming has long been the main occupation of San Felipe Pueblo, a demand for the intricate beadwork that is the specialty of the San Felipe women has created a new business opportunity for the Pueblo's talented artisans. Additionally, the Pueblo's casino has recently begun to bring more significant revenue into the community. These revenues have made it possible for the Pueblo to build a new elementary school, create a Head Start program and center for the elderly, and establish health and social programs.

Like other Pueblo Indians, Esther Tenorio, Guidance Coordinator of the Santa Fe Indian School, appreciates the complexity of living in "two worlds." From her father, Frank Tenorio, former San Felipe governor, she learned how important it is "to know how to utilize what the two worlds we live in have to offer and to be creative to reap the rewards of both cultures." She says that, like others, she was "taught through hard work, prayer, and sacrifice." Her father told her: "No one walks by himself. There is always a spirit who is with us and protects us."

Sara Candelaria with her sister

Pot by Darrell Candelaria

San Felipe's Casino Hollywood

Frank Tenorio

Darrell Candelaria with his pottery

San Ildefonso

Clara Montoya

Maria Martinez

Darlene Martinez

Indian Name: Po-who-ge/O weenge: "Where the Water Cuts Through"

Language: Tewa

Feast Day: January 23

Location: 25 miles north of Santa Fe

Area: 26,198 acres   Population: 725

Juan Cruz Roybal

Deer Dance

Ancestors of this Pueblo people may have built the villages at Bandelier National Monument, near present-day Los Alamos, New Mexico. The present town is a little north of the site where it stood about A.D. 1300. Once the residents drew water for irrigation from the Pojoaque River and collaborated in farming with people in a town just across the river. These two towns probably merged and became the foundation of the modern-day Pueblo, now listed as a historic district on the National Register of Historic Places.

At the time of contact with the Spanish, San Ildefonso was the largest of the Tewa pueblos. The people of San Ildefonso fought the Spanish in the Pueblo Revolt of 1680 and battled against them again in later conflicts, frequently taking refuge on their sacred Black Mesa, which stands north of San Ildefonso. Over the years, conflict and disease caused the population to plummet until there were barely a hundred people in the Pueblo after World War I. The Spanish Flu epidemic in 1918 was particularly devastating to the Pueblo people.

As the Native population decreased, squatters began to move onto San Ildefonso lands, gradually pushing the Pueblo people into the drier, upland portion of their reservation, where farming was very difficult. The Pueblo people began to turn to other means of support, including traditional crafts and wage jobs in Santa Fe or Los Alamos. Though the younger generations of San Ildefonso's people leave the Pueblo for education or work, the link to home is strong. Tim Roybal, a scholarship student at Denver University, says, "With my family and friends behind me, it makes sense for me to work as hard as I can in college so I can come back and help my family and my community."

Tim Roybal is an artist whose work has already won awards; he comes from a family of artists, including his grandfather, J. D. Roybal. "My grandfather's style was very traditional, with geometric dance figures. I've adopted some of his techniques and added my own style, using the airbrush, a toothbrush, and stencils to render both abstract designs and figures. I don't want to stay with just one style."

For Tim Roybal, as for all Pueblo people, the roots of home go deep. "Home is where the heart is," Tim says. "My great grandfather used to tell me, and my dad still tells me: 'Know who you are and where you come from, because that's the most important part of your identity.'"

Buffalo and Deer Dance

San Ildefonso's success in pottery has been spectacular, and its most famous exponent was Maria Martinez. Around the turn of the century, archaeologists and scholars asked Maria to duplicate the ancient technique and designs of the intriguing black-on-black fragments of ancient Tewa pottery that had been excavated from the ruins of a prehistoric pueblo. She did so, and then quickly developed her own designs for pottery, which people much admired and copied. Her husband, Julian, joined her in making the pottery. Maria was the first Native potter in the

Julia Roybal

South kiva

Southwest to sign her work, which has become highly collectible today. Their son Popovi Da carried on the family tradition at San Ildefonso, developing new glazes and a polychrome technique that have been adopted by many other potters. Today the works of Blue Corn, another San Ildefonso potter, are considered representative of the finest of this style.

In a speech, Popovi Da described the Native views about art: "Our culture and our creative arts are interwoven and inseparable. . . . To be able to use our symbols and keep in harmony with our world we must work by fasting, continence, solitary vigil, and symbolic discipline. Out of the silences of meditation come purity and power which eventually become apparent in our art."

San Ildefonso drummers

Darlene Martinez as "Malinche" in the Matachina Dance

Those who behold the artwork of Native peoples are also witnessing a spiritual expression, and this is what gives it its capacity to speak so eloquently to so many people.

The Pueblo of San Ildefonso sometimes hosts the annual Northern Pueblos Artist and Craftsman Show.

Above: Lucy and Richard Martinez making and firing their pottery

Maria Martinez

Carrying saints back to the church

Darlene Martinez

Gary Roybal with son, Tim

Lucy Martinez

142

Black Mesa

San Ildefonso recently returned to electing its governor and council in the traditional way. The Feast Day of San Ildefonso on January 23 is an occasion for Buffalo and Comanche Dances, and visitors are welcome to gather in the plaza, in the shade of the huge 200-year-old cottonwood tree, to witness them. Tim Roybal says, "The dances are prayers of thankfulness, in appreciation for all the life here on earth. We dance to give thanks, and to maintain our identity. If we didn't do these dances or take part in the ceremonies, our lives would be without meaning."

Leon Roybal of San Ildefonso wrote the following in memory of his father, J. D. Roybal, and his grandfather, Juan Cruz Roybal:

"Now this is the day, my child
Into the daylight you will go out standing
Preparing for your day.
We have passed our days."

The late J. D. Roybal

After the Corn Dance, dancers gather to remember relatives who have passed.

145

Renee Roybal and Bernice Martinez

Above: Darrylinn Martinez

Below: Sonja Roybal

Above: Sonja Roybal, Darlene Martinez, and Darrylinn Martinez

Below: Playing on the plaza

147

Desiree Roybal

Blue Corn with her grandchild 149

Adam and Santana Martinez

Corn Dance   *Leon Roybal with daughter, Sonja*

San Juan

Peter Garcia

Crucita Atencio

Alfonso Ortiz

Ester Martinez

Indian Name: Ohkay Owingeh: "Place of the Strong People" or
"We are the Brothers"

Language: Tewa

Feast Day: June 24

Location: On the Rio Grande, just north of Española

Area: 12,238 acres   *Population:* 1,806

Though about one hundred of the houses at San Juan Pueblo are centuries old, the cottonwood-shaded village is more distinguished for its role in the larger Pueblo community than for its architecture. A neighbor of the Tanoan pueblos Picuris and Taos and culturally related to them, San Juan has long been a political leader. In 1598 the Spanish established their first New Mexico capital across the river in San Gabriel and renamed the Pueblo San Juan de los Caballeros. (Ten years later they moved the capital to Santa Fe.)

The 1680 Pueblo Revolt may have originated at San Juan. Fed up with the Spanish abuses of forced labor, suppression of religion, and constant violent requisitions of food and other supplies, leaders of the Pueblos began to meet and envision a united Pueblo people who would drive the Spanish out. At San Juan, an important Pueblo man named Popé helped in the organization. Tradition has it that he was one of the leaders of the revolt. Momentum toward the overthrow of the Spanish slowly built in the kivas of the pueblos below the Sangre de Cristo Mountains. Gradually other villages were drawn into the plan, and a scheme was devised. On the same day in mid-August, within each Pueblo the people were to ask the Spanish to leave. If they refused, the Pueblos would attack them. Knotted deer hide strips were sent to each participating pueblo to mark the passage of the days. The plan was discovered, however, and the Indians had to advance the action by two days.

The revolt began at Tesuque on August 10, 1680, where the priest Fray Juan Pio was killed, and at Taos, where the Pueblos fell on Spanish settlers in the area, killing seventy immediately. Other pueblos followed suit. The remaining Spanish fled to the Governor's Palace at Santa Fe, where they were besieged for five days before managing to fight their way out. Once the siege was broken, the Spanish continued south, abandoning all they had built and fleeing for their lives. They stayed away for only about a dozen years, in the interim making repeated efforts at reconquest, which finally succeeded in 1692. The Pueblos made subsequent attempts to overthrow the Spanish again, especially in 1694 and 1696, but these failed. In a few years, as more Spanish families arrived with their sheep and cattle, and raids by the Plains tribes increased, the Pueblos and the Spanish began to work together to protect themselves. The relations between the two groups were changed forever.

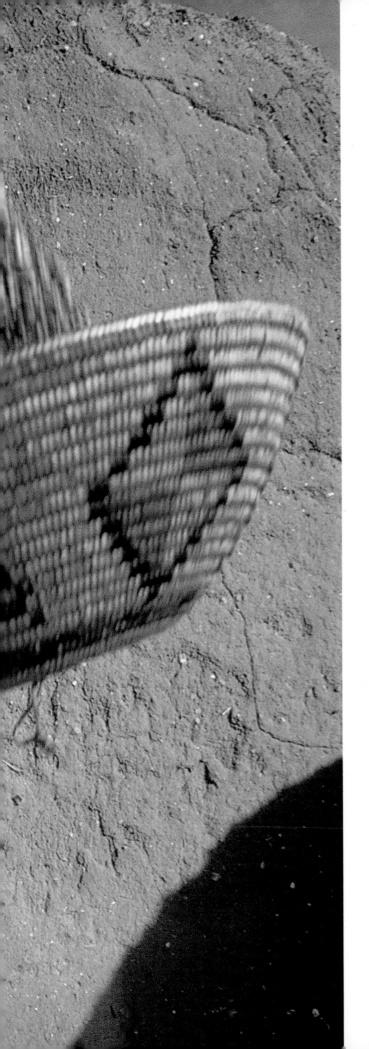

Today San Juan is the administrative seat of the Eight Northern Indian Pueblos Council. San Juan pottery is justly famous and provides good income for its makers; the casino is also a source of revenue for the Pueblo.

San Juan, through its agriculture cooperative called Ohkay T'owa Gardens, is reintroducing traditional Pueblo farming and providing Pueblo-produced and packaged food products to northern New Mexico communities. These products include dried green chile stew, roasted dried green sweet corn, dried tomatoes smoked with apple wood, and various soup mixes, which are sold in health food stores.

Saint John's Feast Day

Crucita Atencio

157

Several hundred acres of fields beyond the Pueblo are under cultivation, and the chilies and tomatoes grown there are sun-dried in a solar greenhouse and sold to local health food stores. The greenhouse, provided by Sandia National Laboratories in Albuquerque, is an example of adapting modern technology to serve traditional purposes, helping the tribe to maintain its agricultural way of life.

The Pueblo has also provided scholars and professionals to the world. The late Alfonso Ortiz, the distinguished anthropologist, was a member of San Juan Pueblo.

Like other Tanoan pueblos, San Juan Pueblo is divided into Summer and Winter People. They use two rectangular kivas built into house blocks for their ceremonial activities. There are also Basket Dances, Buffalo Dances, and a Cloud Dance.

Geronima Archuleta

Alfonso Ortiz

Ester Martinez

Peter Garcia, a San Juan Pueblo resident, has played a major role in keeping San Juan's traditional dances alive. In the 1950s, he committed himself to studying the ancient dances and learning the Tewa songs and stories from the elders, writing them down in English. He is spending the rest of his life passing on this heritage to the younger generations. "I gave my life over to teaching the songs, stories, and dances," he says. "I was doing it for the spirits, and they helped, giving me their powers and telling me what to do."

Plastering Alfonso Ortiz' house

Peter Garcia

Nathan Garcia

Because elders like Peter Garcia have devoted themselves to the preservation of their traditions, today, on the Feast Day of San Juan on June 24 and at other ceremonies during the year, the plaza is as full of dancers as it might have been centuries ago.

Next pages: Deer Dance

Left: Reyecita Garcia with her grandchildren

Top Left: Curtis Aquino

Top Right: Alfred Chavez and Belen Aguilar

Bottom Left: David Calabaza and son

Bottom Right: Lorenzo Aquino

Next pages:
Buffalo Dancers
Nolan Cruz and Danny Garcia

Santa Ana

Elveria Montoya

Donna Pino

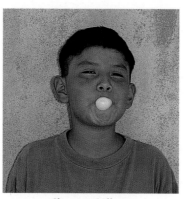

Clarence Gallegos

Indian name: Tamaya

Language: Keres

Feast Day: July 26

Location: 10 miles northwest of Bernalillo

Area: 44,589 acres   Population: 533

Vonda Gallegos

Santa Ana Pueblo was evidently off the beaten Spanish track, as little is recorded of it during the period of initial contact. It is clear, however, that the people of Santa Ana, known as the Tamayame, suffered from the Spanish imposition of forced labor, proscription of religious practices, and requisitioning of food and other supplies, because the people of this pueblo retaliated by joining in the Pueblo Revolt in 1680.

Present-day Santa Ana is a reconstituted pueblo. Much of its original land was lost after the village was abandoned following the Pueblo Revolt. Many members of Santa Ana were killed, and the rest left, searching for a more secure place to live. After the Spanish reconquest, surviving people from old Santa Ana returned and founded the present-day Pueblo in a new location in the 1700s. Since the land "granted" to the Pueblo by the Spanish decree of 1687 was not large enough to grow sufficient food for the village or to pasture their increasing herds of livestock, the Pueblo gradually bought back some of their ancestral lands from Spanish settlers, making a number of purchases during the eighteenth century. This struggle has continued into the present century, as the Santa Ana people have pursued a daunting series of legal actions in an effort to regain access to their traditional pastures. The lands around the Pueblo are dry, and the Jemez River on which it is situated has tended, in the past, to flood. Today the river is controlled by a dam built in 1952.

Not much remains of the traditional pueblo structures of Santa Ana. Its relatively few people now live mostly in modern homes on the reservation at Ranchito, north of Bernalillo. Some Santa Ana Pueblo people farm and others pursue more urban professions, but there has also been a renaissance of traditional crafts on the Pueblo. Once again, Santa Anans can earn a living making pottery and woven goods, particularly belts and handbags.

Jean Robbins, a Santa Ana resident, works in Albuquerque but also makes pottery. She lived for a time in California but was never happy off the reservation. "Now we're back home and I would never leave it again," she says. "The Indian way of life is irreplaceable. To the Indian everything is sacred, from the earth to the sky. The white man's viewpoint about the earth is curiosity—'what can be done with this to increase my wealth?' But for the Indian, the earth and everything on it IS wealth. Even the leftover clay

Roy Montoya

Santa Ana nursery

from a pot is usable, precious. We can make something from it."

Santa Ana runs a casino, and Jean Robbins says the gambling revenue has benefitted the Pueblo. "They have renovated many society houses (kivas), built a new library, an addition to the Head Start building that also houses the senior center, a tribal police building, and bought new police cars. It's brought a lot of jobs to the village. So I think a lot of good has come out of it."

Raymond Coriz ploughing

Santa Ana Star Casino

Traditionally, Santa Ana people were organized into two kiva groups, the Squash or Pumpkin People and the Turquoise People; each group had its own kiva for ritual purposes. The people also were traditionally subdivided into clans and medicine societies. A single cacique serves the people for a lifetime.

Despite their modernized lifestyles, Santa Ana people gather in large numbers at the traditional village of Tamaya to celebrate feast days, when urban dwellers return home and hold the Corn Dance and other dances. The Corn Dance that marks the annual feast of Santa Ana (Saint Anne) on July 26 is always heavily attended, and for a day or two, the Pueblo regains the atmosphere of the past.

Evangelina Leon

Besides the casino, other modern enterprises of Santa Ana Pueblo include a championship twenty-seven-hole golf course, the Santa Ana Garden Center, and the Prairie Star restaurant. These businesses employ many Pueblo members and have helped to revitalize the Santa Ana community.

Diane Menchego

Art Menchego

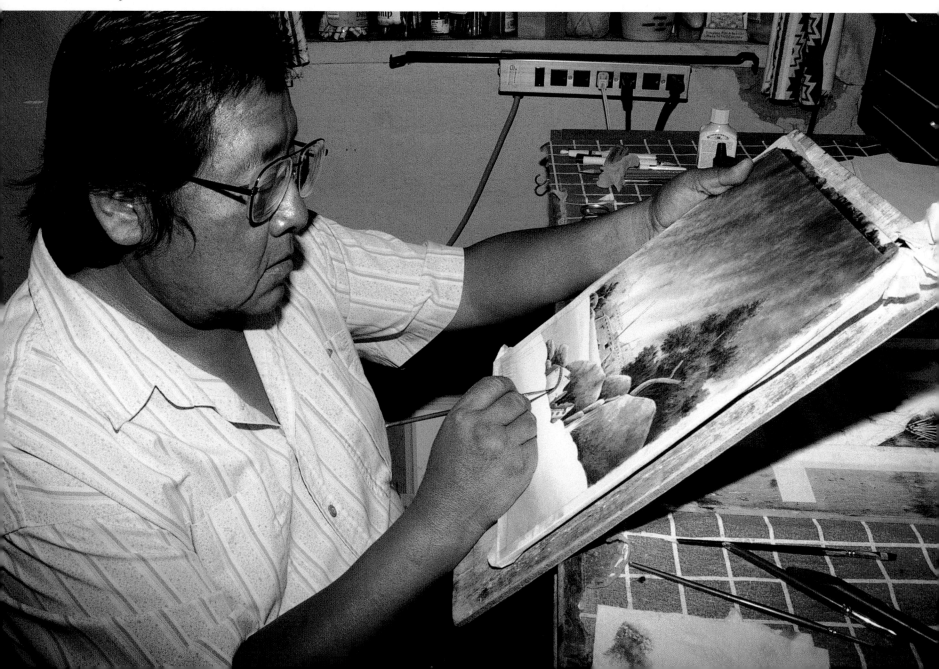

Vonda Gallegos

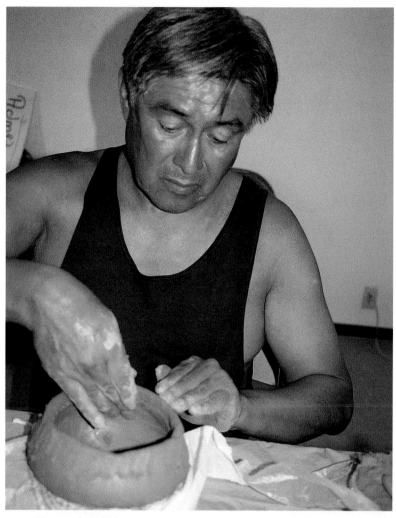

Donna Pino

Above: Adam Montoya

Below: Annette Raton

Santa Clara

Pablita Velarde

Trisha Dasheno

Alexandria Dasheno

Indian Name: Kha P'o: "Singing Water"

Language: Tewa

Feast Day: August 12

Location: A mile and a half south of Española

Area: 45,746 acres   Population: 1,374

John Jenkins

Entering kiva at end of dance

The ancestors of the Santa Clara Pueblo people built the two and three story apartment buildings of the nearby Puye Cliff dwellings, and they lived there until sometime in the early 1500s. Today, those ruins have been listed as a National Historic Landmark and are maintained as a public monument by the Santa Clara Pueblo, which, like all the pueblos, has a strong sense of its own history.

Santa Clara participated in the Pueblo Revolt of 1680; a Santa Claran of mixed African and native parentage named Domingo Naranjo was one of the revolt's leaders. The Pueblo rebelled again in 1696, and afterward its people fled the village. In one of history's ironies, a son of Domingo Naranjo named Joseph Naranjo became an ally of the Spanish, and it was he who eventually persuaded some Santa Clara people to return to their pueblo. His brother Lucas, the leader of the 1696 revolt, was killed at the battle of Embudo.

Traditionally, Santa Clara Pueblo people are divided into Summer and Winter People. Each group has a rectangular kiva in which they hold sacred activities, but the Pueblo organizes other religious functions under a single cacique. The Pueblo elects its governor and council; Santa Clara was the first pueblo to adopt a constitution, in December 1935.

Today Santa Clarans are employed in businesses on and off the reservation. Santa Clara pottery, both black on black, and red and black, is quite distinctive, being made of very hard clay that takes a deep shine when polished and that may be sculpted into bas-relief designs before firing. Tessie Naranjo, a member of a family of potters, says, "It's important for the potter to gather his or her own clay. That's when the potter's sacred relationship with the clay begins. The potter prays to the Clay Lady for help and guidance before gathering the clay. The earth has life—and the clay is a part of the earth."

The Pueblo operates the Santa Clara Recreation Area, which has four lakes and twelve miles of Santa Clara Creek available for fishing, camping, and picnicking. The Pueblo offers a variety of dances that are open to the public.

Pablita Velarde, an internationally known artist from Santa Clara, has described the dances: "At sunrise the dancers come down from the hills, led into the village by the priests. The women go down the road to meet them, and as they pass by they sprinkle sacred cornmeal on the dancers and ask for blessings. The dance is one of thanksgiving, thanking the spirit of the animal whose antlers they are wearing for giving us food from their flesh.

At the end of the day of dancing, the deer and the mountain sheep, the elk and the antelopes are turned loose in the plaza and then the ladies chase them and whoever catches one takes the dancer home, and they feed him and give him meat to take home to his family to show appreciation. It is an honor to catch a wild deer."

The Pueblo's governor, Walter Dasheno, says, "We have lost some of our ways, but not all. As long as we maintain our language, our laws, and our customs, we will be able to sustain our values and carry out our responsibility to Mother Earth and to each other."

Corn Dances and Buffalo Dances are performed in June and on the Pueblo's feast day, August 12.

Roxanne Swentzel's clay sculpture

Tessie Naranjo with her niece

Roxanne Swentzel

C. C. Naranjo between dances

Upper left: *Trisha Dasheno with her grandfather, Carl Tsosie*
Lower left: *Judy Dasheno with her daughter, Alex*
Lower right: *Aurelia Lente with her granddaughter, Kara*

Right: *Pablita Velarde with her granddaughter, Helen*

Pablita Velarde

Joseph Abeyta Jr., Superintendent of Santa Fe Indian School

Harvest Dance

Rose Naranjo

Julia Roybal with her sisters, Bea Chavarria & Aurelia Lente

Blessing the fields in the Spring

Next pages: Harvest Dance

Santo Domingo

Gilbert Pacheco

Lorenzo Tortalita

Yaya Ortiz

Robert Tenerio

Indian Name: Kewa

Language: Keres

Feast Day: August 4

Location: 25 miles south of Santa Fe

Area: 69,260 acres   Population: 2,971

Wedding feast

The Santo Domingo people can trace their roots a long way back into the ancient Southwest. They may be directly descended from the people of Chaco Canyon. Some of the Chaco Canyon people may have moved to the area of what is now Bandelier National Monument, before establishing themselves in their present location.

Spanish colonizers, led by Don Juan de Oñate, found the Santo Domingo people along the Rio Grande in 1598, where he met thirty-eight Pueblo leaders officially for the first time on July 7, 1598. (This meeting was repeated on July 7, 1998, by delegates from Spain and local Franciscan priests.) Oñate quickly put the Pueblo people to work as reluctant, unpaid servants farming for the Spanish and tending their livestock and gardens. Drought made this harsh regime worse. The Spanish seized Santo Domingo's and other pueblos' meager stores, causing widespread starvation among the Native people. The viceroy, angered by stories of Oñate's cruelty and the general disarray of the colony, recalled Oñate to Mexico City in 1610, leaving the Pueblo people to rebuild their disrupted society.

The Santo Domingo people, who had initially not been hostile to the Spanish, tried to have as little as possible to do with them when they returned to the New Mexico area. They were committed participants in the Pueblo Revolt of 1680. A Santo Domingan named Alonzo Catiti led his pueblo and the rest of the Keres into battle, and is said to have celebrated with a victory banquet in which he drank a mock-European-style toast with Popé, the revolt's chief leader. Santo Domingan people continued their resistance during the period of Spanish reconquest that began in 1692.

Even today, Santo Domingo, like the Keresan-speaking pueblo of San Felipe, guards its traditions and seeks to maintain its time-distilled way of life. The village is composed of an assortment of adobe and modern houses grouped around a large plaza that is anchored by a white-washed mission church, brightly decorated with geometric designs. Like other Keresan peoples, the Pueblo is divided into the Squash or Pumpkin People and Turquoise People. The kiva groups use the Pueblo's two round kivas, and a single cacique serves as religious leader.

Principal occupations here are farming, hunting, and jewelry making. The Santo Domingo people are well known for their turquoise and silver jewelry and heishe (carved stone or shell)

Connie and Evelino Calabaza
at their wedding

necklaces. A productive turquoise mine, Los Cerrillos, is located near the Pueblo, and the Santo Domingans have had long experience trading turquoise stones and jewelry for other valuable commodities such as eagle and parrot feathers and pottery and baskets. Santo Domingans are tireless traders still, traveling widely to sell the Pueblo's distinctive jewelry, and their efforts have succeeded in making Santo Domingo one of the best-known pueblos in the world beyond New Mexico.

Santo Domingo's pottery is often characterized by highly traditional adaptations of classic red and white designs that date to the 1700s. Not all of its potters, however, feel bound by tradition. William Pacheco, the son of two distinguished potters from Santo Domingo, Gilbert and Paulita Pacheco, and a graduate of the University of New Mexico, applies a thoroughly modern technique. He initially drafts his designs on the computer, then executes them on the pot using the classic glazes, and finally fires and polishes them in the time-honored manner. Gilbert's approach is characteristic of so many Pueblo Indians; he selects what he wants from the modern world and freely combines it with the ancient ways he chooses to maintain.

The Pueblo's own Santo Domingo Arts and Crafts Market, held on Labor Day, is a spectacular shopping opportunity accompanied by dances and traditional food. A Corn Dance, on August 4, usually attracts an impressive number of participants, who fill the large plaza with the thunder of drumming and dancing feet.

One of seven truckloads of wedding presents

199

William Pacheco

Deer is honored with jewelry in many houses

William Pacheco's dinosaur pot

Margaret Tenorio with her granddaughter

Gilbert Pacheco with granddaughter, Shavelle

Caroline Martinez cooking

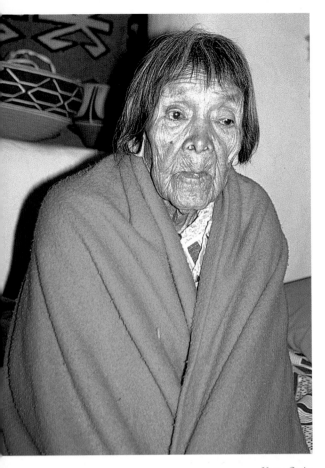

Yaya Ortiz

Lolita Crespin with her son Tenzen

Evelino and Connie's wedding shower

Robert Tenerio with pot

Internationally known potter Robert Tenerio lives and works in the Pueblo. "I do pottery in the old style using the traditional techniques of clay gathering and firing," he says. "I no longer look for perfection. Whatever comes out of the firing—that's the result. The firing is the final judgment day. I do pottery as art but pots are meant to be used. I enjoy serving food in them on feast days."

Robert Tenerio at work

Benny Atencio

Jerry & Madeline Nieto

Gilbert Pacheco

Paulita and Gilbert Pacheco

Angie Owen

Jewelry by Angie Owen

Hilda Coriz

Taos

Tony Reyna

Leandro Bernal

Marlene Reyna Platero

Indian Name: Tua-tah: "Our Village"

Language: Northern Tiwa

Feast Day: San Geronimo Day, September 30

Location: One mile north of the town of Taos

Area: 95,341 acres   *Population:* 1,951

Frank C. Romero

Taos Pueblo, the largest multistory pueblo structure in the United States and the best known and most-photographed symbol of Pueblo culture, was built about 500 years ago in the valley below the Sangre de Cristo Mountains. The builders of Taos had lived in the Taos Valley for a thousand years, and before that perhaps had lived in southwestern Colorado, west of Cortez. When they arrived at the site of the present pueblo, they found the valley lush with wildlife and the Rio Pueblo flowing down from Blue Lake in the mountains.

Taos is the northernmost of the pueblos, and this isolation enabled it to avoid some of the most egregious Spanish demands for forced labor and supplies, and to maintain its independent beliefs. The first mission church was built there in the early 1600s and destroyed soon after, during a revolt in 1639 brought on by Catholic priests' attempts to ban traditional Pueblo practices. This action in many ways foreshadowed the Pueblo Revolt of 1680, in which the Pueblo people ousted the Spanish for a time.

Because of its northerly position, Apaches, Utes, and later Comanches frequently raided Taos Pueblo as well as the nearby Spanish villages.

With its powerful adobe walls, Taos became the fortress refuge for all in the region, who would crowd together inside for defense against the marauders from the plains.

Taos Pueblo has been constructed of adobe (mud and straw) bricks in two great blocks that face each other across the Rio Pueblo. The river bisects the center of the plaza and provides fresh water for the townspeople and their livestock. In order to maintain the traditional style of living, the Taos people have chosen to live without electricity or running water within the walls of the Pueblo. This choice does not mean that Taos Pueblo people refuse to be modern in any way. Some may live a traditional life at home and yet are perfectly comfortable working with computers, lasers, and cellular telephones. Those who prefer modern conveniences live in houses nearby on the reservation, outside the walls. Taos Pueblo has yielded many well-respected scientists, physicians, educators, and artists.

The people of Taos Pueblo traditionally belong to either one of two groups: The North Side or the South Side People. This symbolic division is a traditional feature of the Tanoan culture group, of which Taos Pueblo is a part. Each group has its

Henry Montoya exercising his horses

own spiritual leader, or cacique. There are six kivas in Taos Pueblo, each surrounded by a palisade of poles, and another kiva outside the village.

Dances and ceremonies open to the public include the Taos Pow Wow in July and San Geronimo's Feast Day on September 30. Pole climbing and war dances are featured at the San Geronimo Feast. Other activities on that day include ceremonial races. The racetrack stretches east to west, and the foot races held there are intended to empower the sun and moon. The North and South Sides compete by racing back and forth in relays. Tony Reyna, a former governor of Taos, says, "In the afternoon there's a pole climbing. We have what we call 'Koshare the clown' who makes people laugh by imitating them or making them perform dances. The Koshare must climb the pole, which is about 75 feet high. There are some gifts representing the harvest on top of the pole, and one clown goes up and brings them down. People down below grab

him and make fun of the situation." Tony Reyna says, "We have approximately one hundred head of buffalo here and have either a deer or a Buffalo Dance every January. It's a beautiful dance, performed in the afternoon and lasting a couple of hours."

The people of Taos have had to face many struggles to maintain their land and culture. The threats to their native religion began with the Spanish missionaries and continued into the present century. In 1926 an Indian Affairs official told the people of Taos they were "half animals"

Leandro Bernal

because of their "pagan religion," which he ordered them to give up "within a year." The Taos elders responded, "Our happiness, our moral behavior, our unity as a people, and the peace and joyfulness of our homes, are all a part of our religion and are dependent on its continuation. To pass this religion, with its hidden sacred knowledge and its many forms of prayer, on to our children, is our supreme duty to our ancestors and to our own hearts and to the God whom we know."

Taos Pueblo fought another battle over one of its most sacred sites, Blue Lake, serene and sky-bound among the mountains above the Pueblo. For hundreds of years, the people of Taos had observed ceremonies of the utmost secrecy at this lake, which they believe to be the place of their emergence as a people and the place to which they will return after death. But in 1906 President Theodore Roosevelt signed an order that made Blue Lake and the area around it into part of a national forest. The objections of the people of Taos were ignored, and grazing permits were handed out to non-Indians that allowed them to trespass at will on the sacred site. Non-Indians were allowed to hike and camp at Blue Lake year round while the Taos people were allowed a mere

Quirino Romero

Carpio Bernal

three days to observe their religious practices, provided they gave the authorities ten days' notice! Taos Pueblo's people, supported eventually by all the other pueblos, other Indians, and by a growing contingent of non-Indian Americans, continued to press their case. Some ten bills failed in Congress before the passage of the Harris-Griffin bill in 1970 that, after more than sixty years, returned Blue Lake to its rightful owners. The victory of the people of Taos Pueblo was one of the most significant instances in American history of an indigenous people reclaiming its traditional rights.

The people of Taos make their living from traditional crafts like blankets, drums, deer-skin moccasins, jewelry, and micaceous pottery, and from contemporary off-reservation jobs. The Pueblo runs a casino that has contributed substantially to its collective income. The revenues are being used to pay for sacred land previously confiscated by the federal government.

Taos Pueblo is listed on the National Register of Historic Places.

The people of the Pueblo value education and see it as a key to the future. Tony Reyna says, "My granddaughter just graduated from MIT and is heading for Stanford University in California. That indicates the growth of the intellectual area for Pueblo people. We need to learn more, but also to apply it in accordance with our traditional values."

Reyna's granddaughter Marlene is keenly aware of the juggling act this implies. She intends to do research in ceramics and electronics materials, and knows that for this work she will probably have to live away from Taos for a while. "But this is my home and my people," she says. "This is where I feel comfortable. It hurts to miss my feast day, but what I am doing at MIT is part of something that is also important for Native American people." She hopes to be able to

Blue Lake Celebration 1991

Tony Reyna

Blue Lake Celebration 1971

work at her profession for perhaps ten or fifteen years. "And then I'm going to come home, either to teach or to work in the environmental office." Like many other Pueblo people, she hopes to combine old and new, traditional and contemporary ways. The effort to do this must be reinvented by each person who undertakes to walk this dual path.

Left: Ronnie Martinez with son Tony
Below: Taking horses home
Right: Cindy and Melanie blowing bubbles

222

Top left: Teresino Jiron
Top right: Mr. Lucero
Below: Old church and cemetery

Taos buffalo herd

Above: Ursula Mirabal
Right: Tony Martinez with his grandmother

The sacred Blue Lake provides the precious water that keeps Pueblo land fertile and green. Taos resident Rose Marie Cordova describes walking near her home: "I walk along a road with aspen trees on either side. A large mountain looms ahead. I think of it as an altar. I see a cornfield lush and green, gifts from our creator. I feel blessed."

Pete Concha

Tesuque

Priscilla Vigil

Vickie Downey

Tom Tapia

Indian name: Te-Tsu-Geh: "Cottonwood Tree Place"

Language: Tewa

Feast Day: November 12

Location: 9 miles north of Santa Fe

Area: 16,813 acres   *Population:* 312

Terrence Pino

Eagle dancers

Tesuque is surprisingly traditional for a pueblo so close to Santa Fe, but its people have managed to maintain their culture through their reverence for religion and the cohesiveness of the Pueblo's small population of approximately three hundred people. In fact, the Pueblo is so small that visitors sometimes think it is deserted.

Tesuque has apparently never been large, even before the arrival of the Spanish; Coronado estimated its population at 170. The Tesuque Valley had been settled since A.D. 800, and Natives had built large pueblos there by the 1300s. The farmers of Tesuque have long been dependent on irrigation to make their dry fields fruitful.

Tesuque played a prominent role in the Pueblo Revolt of 1680. Just before the revolt, the Spanish governor, Otermìn, captured two Tesuque messengers, and on the day it began, the people of the Pueblo murdered Fray Juan Baptista Pio as he arrived to hold mass. His guard managed to escape and notify the Spanish that the revolt had begun. Tesuque Pueblo's people participated in the siege of Santa Fe but were persuaded not to engage in further hostilities when the Spanish returned during the reconquest period twelve years later.

The people of Tesuque Pueblo have traditionally been farmers, but the increased water demands of non-Indian settlers nearby had diminished the water supply needed for irrigation and farming. The Traditional Native American Farmer's Association, founded by Clayton Brascoupe and his wife Margaret Vigil and their children, provides for training in growing traditional native seed stock, to insure that all varieties of food crops that the Pueblos traditionally enjoyed, such as squash, corn, and beans, will exist for future generations. The association works with the agriculture extension service as well as the pueblos and southwest regional organizations focused on preserving dry land seed stock.

Most Tesuque people make their living in Santa Fe or Los Alamos, or through traditional crafts such as pottery, drums, and beadwork, and other arts such as sculpture and painting. Like many other pueblos, Tesuque has a casino. Revenue from the casino has allowed Tesuque to improve its school and establish scholarships for its students. The plaza and some of the substandard homes have been renovated, allowing more people to return to live at the Pueblo.

Tesuque drummers

Marita Hinds with her daughter, Cienna Giago

The village of low adobe buildings maintains a very traditional appearance. Tesuque Pueblo has a dual division of Summer People and Winter People, who use two rectangular kivas, built into house blocks, for religious activities.

Tesuque Pueblo is governed by two caciques; one represents the Summer and one the Winter People. Tesuque's annual feast day is celebrated on November 12 in honor of San Diego. That festival, and Deer and Buffalo Dances in December, are open to the public and attended by many people. Tesuque Pueblo is listed on the National Register of Historic Places.

Spring cleaning

Priscilla Vigil with her daughter Vicky Downey & granddaughter Teressa

Priscilla Vigil, a grandmother and elder, said, "The parents are the first teachers. My parents taught me the importance of loving myself, and in that way I would love other people, and not lose my prayers and my Tewa ways. If the children are given the good foundation and the tradi-tional way of life in the home they grow up in, they are not lost and they make a good life for themselves. The prayers and dances make us who we are. I say a lot of prayers and pray to the Great Spirit."

Comanche Dance

234

Comanche Dance in the snow

Tesuque church

Jerome Martinez with his new wife, Pauline

Right: Comanche Dance

Zia

Helen Gachupin

Peter Pino

Lois Medina

Indian Name: Tsia

Language: Keres

Feast Day: August 15

Location: 18 miles northwest of Bernalillo

Area: 112,533 acres   Population: 676

Rafael Medina

Zia Pueblo tops a volcanic butte along the Jemez River in particularly gorgeous terrain. The dry landscape, dotted with trees, has sweeping views of the Pajarito and Jemez Plateaus. The beauty of the Zia reservation is one reason that Hollywood westerns are sometimes filmed here, with the encouragement of the Pueblo people.

Zia, founded in the thirteenth century, was not always idyllic, however. The Spanish arrived in the sixteenth century, and subjected the Zia people to the encomienda, a forced labor and taxation system. They also proscribed the Native religious practices, and severely punished those who persisted. The Zia people participated in the Pueblo Revolt of 1680 with zeal, temporarily driving the Spanish away. In 1689 a new Spanish governor, Domingo Petrez de Cruzate, visited the Pueblo region and attacked Zia. Six hundred of Zia's residents were killed and the village itself was burned and leveled by the Spanish. The survivors fled to the mountains west of Jemez or to other pueblos for safety. In 1692, Diego de Vargas, the Spanish commander who led the reconquest, ordered that Zia should be rebuilt.

Zia is not among the largest in terms of population, but it has recovered substantially since the late nineteenth century, when conflict with the Navajo and epidemics, particularly smallpox, had reduced it to about one hundred people. The Pueblo as a whole earns income from leasing real estate. Zia's 750 people do a little farming (the region is very dry), raise livestock, work outside of the Pueblo, and pursue their traditional crafts. The people of Zia Pueblo have for a long time made a uniquely painted and very hard pottery from red clay covered with a white slip and painted in black and white designs. One favorite motif is the "Zia bird," an alert-looking roadrunner.

The present-day town stands on the site of the original pueblo. The road to Zia Pueblo winds up the butte, past low modern buildings, and up to the village of more traditional stone and adobe buildings. Two round kivas in the Pueblo provide shelter for the ceremonies of the two traditional kiva groups, the Wren People and the Turquoise People. In the custom of Zia, its people are also divided into clan groups, and a child is born into the clan of his or her mother.

Street scene

Sophie Medina

Rio Grande

The village of Zia is crowned by a water tower with a distinctive symbol. If this red-circled golden sun with its bold red rays looks familiar, it should. This Zia symbol was adopted in the 1920s as the symbol for New Mexico, and it now appears on the flag, license plates, and other official state items. Small Zia Pueblo's ancient design is now familiar throughout the country.

Zia annually celebrates its saint's feast day on August 15. The statue of the Virgin (Nuestra Señora de la Asuncion, or Our Lady of the Assumption) is carried from the mission church and placed in an arbor, where it receives offerings and then is honored by traditional dances.

Rafael Medina

Lois Medina

Helen Gachupin

Zuni

Governor Robert Lewis

Angie Cellicion

Fernando Cellicion

Mr. Cellicion

Indian name: She-we-na: "The Middle Place"

Language: Zuni

Location: 43 miles south of Gallup

Area: 418,304 acres   Population: 7,754

Corn Mountain

The Zuni people, who call themselves the Ashiwi, have lived in the same region for about 800 years, and were the first Pueblos to have recorded contact with Europeans.

In the spring of 1539, a group of Spaniards led by the Franciscan friar Marcos de Niza headed north from Mexico City toward what they had heard described as seven-storied cities laden with wealth. In the vanguard was Esteban (or Estevanico), a Morrocan-Spaniard who, with three other explorers, had survived a shipwreck and spent seven years wandering among the indigenous peoples of the Southeast and into New Mexico. This experience had given him the reputation for being able to make a successful approach to almost any Indians, known or unknown. Esteban advanced on Zuni, ignoring their warnings not to come closer, and presented himself at Hawikuh, one of the six thriving villages of the Zuni people. In short order, he was stripped of his goods, escorted away, and then killed. Having heard of his death, Fray Marcos turned around and headed back to Mexico, where he reported that he had seen a vast and rich city bigger than Mexico City. Fray Marcos's tale stimulated the expedition the following year of Francisco Vasquez de Coronado.

Forewarned of Coronado's approach, Zuni Pueblo sent its women and children to a safe place nearby and attempted to hold the Pueblo by using bows and arrows against the Spanish guns and metal armor. The Zuni warriors were mowed down, and the Spanish captured Hawikuh. Word went out to all the pueblos of the Zuni defeat. The reception the Spanish received varied from pueblo to pueblo, but they punished any Pueblo hostility or resistance. The Spanish continued into Kansas, and then returned to stay among the pueblos for one more winter. When the Spanish returned empty-handed to Mexico City in 1542, the viceroy was so disappointed with the results of the expedition that he allowed no further incursions into Pueblo country for another thirty-nine years.

When future expeditions did arrive, the Zuni tried to maintain cordiality while keeping the Spanish at a distance, and later invaders, such as Oñate, commented on the tribe's friendliness.

The Zuni participated in the Pueblo Revolt of 1680, and afterward took shelter on their sacred Corn Mountain. They established the present Pueblo soon after.

Geographically isolated and far to the west of most of the New Mexico pueblos, the Zuni were not as much harassed by the Spanish as the pueblos along the Rio Grande. On the other hand, their isolation exposed them more to attack by other tribes. The Zuni often had to defend themselves from Apaches and Navajos and protect their sheep and horses from these raiders. The coming of the railroads brought the most intense incursions on Zuni lands, as developers and settlers coveted and appropriated Zuni property.

Our Lady of Guadalupe Mission Church contains murals of Christian subjects and of kachinas (supernatural beings), the latter painted by Zuni artist Alex Seowtewa. The Zuni Museum Project lets you explore the old village with its dusty streets, adobe walls, and clustered horno ovens (outdoor beehive-shaped ovens—a style borrowed from the Spanish).

The Zuni have specialized in making silver jewelry for over a hundred years. In the late nineteenth century, the Zuni learned silversmithing from a Navajo named Atsidi Chon. They later enriched the jewelry they designed by using first

Governor Robert Lewis, 1965

Governor Robert Lewis, 1995

Olla girl

Mr. Cellicion with drum

turquoise, and then shell, agate, coral, and jet. Zuni jewelry techniques include mosaic channel work, a technique of separating the stones with thin walls of silver, and pettipoint, consisting of many small stones set in silver; the impression is of a mass of semiprecious stones embellished by

silver. About 15 percent of the population—over 1,000 people—are engaged in jewelry making.

The religious leader of the Pueblo is the Bow Clan priest. Zuni Pueblo people elect their governor and council. Zuni Pueblo is divided into clans. There are six kiva groups, one for each of the six directions (including up and down).

One of the most intriguing customs at Zuni is the sacred Shalako dance. The six Shalako kachinas dance on a winter night just before the solstice. Each Shalako dances in a house or a room that has been newly built, decorated with shawls, blankets, and a special altar, and filled with watching people and chanting and drumming singers. Feathers gleam and the wooden beak clacks on the Shalako mask, which makes the dancer taller than a human, as the Shalako sways in time to the rattles shaken by the singers. The dancers and watchers wend their way through the streets from house to house, dancing throughout the night until dawn.

Zuni pictograph

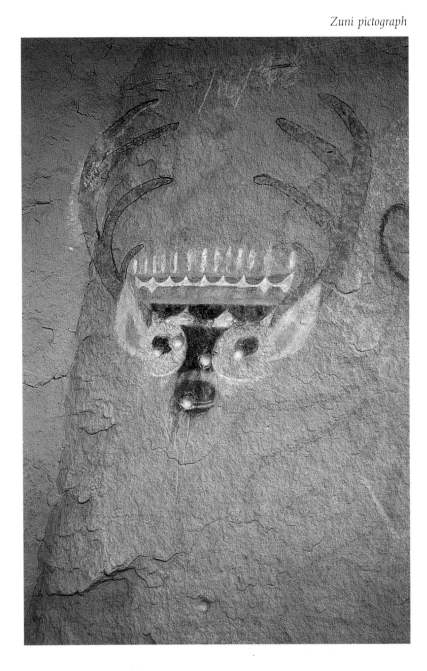

Fernando Cellicion

Zuni church

Buffalo dancers

Angie Cellicion

Thelma Neici making bread

Paul Neici & friend making kachinas

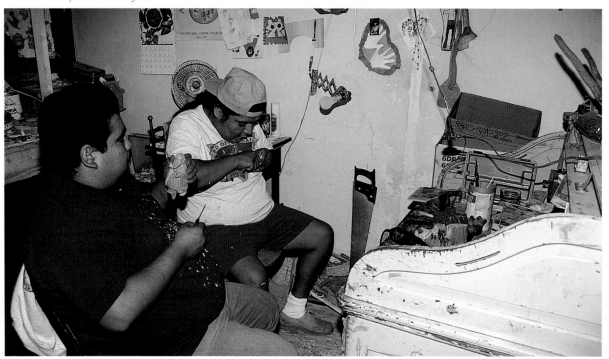

Thelma Neici's grandson in her living room

Zuni pictographs

May we be the ones whom your
        thoughts will embrace,
For this, on this day
        to our sun father,
We offer prayer meal.
To this end:
May you help us
        to finish our roads.

— *Zuni Prayer*

Angie Cellicion & daughter, Calela
Next page: Olla women

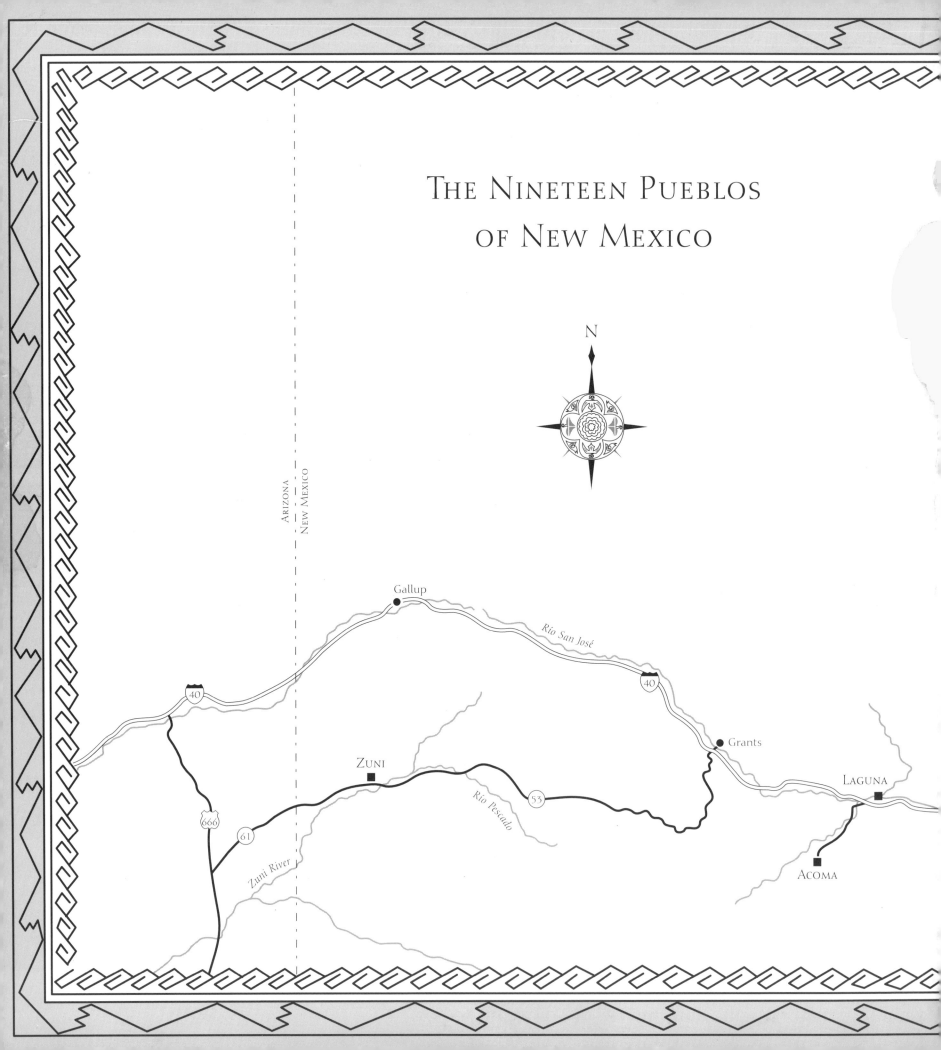

THE NINETEEN PUEBLOS
OF NEW MEXICO

N

ARIZONA
NEW MEXICO

Gallup

Río San José

40

40

Grants

ZUNI

Río Pescado

53

Laguna

666

61

Zuni River

ACOMA